PEOPLES OF THE EARTH

volume twenty

The Future of Mankind

Man past/Man future

THE DANBURY PRESS

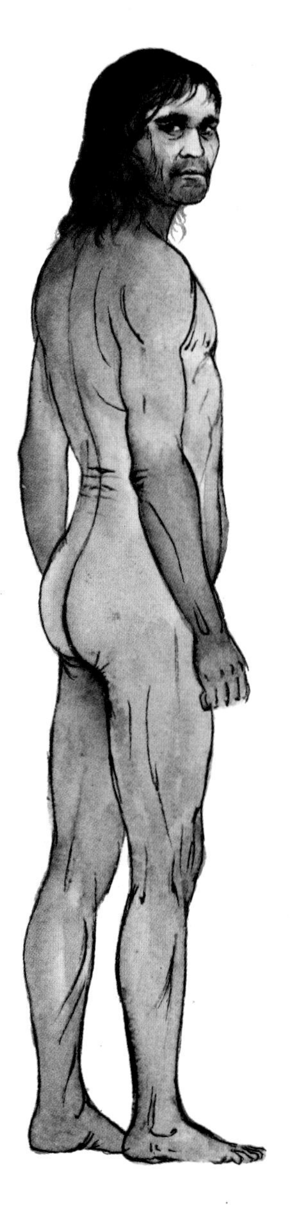

(Preceding page) It is not yet possible to be certain which line of primates led to modern man. Here are shown chronologically (from the left) Australopithecus, Paranthropus, Peking Man (*homo erectus*), Rhodesian Man, Neanderthal Man, Modern Man (*homo sapiens*) and a Spaceman.
Drawings by Maurice Wilson.

Contents

Supervisory Editor of the Series:
Professor Sir Edward Evans-Pritchard,
Fellow of All Souls, Professor of Social Anthropology,
University of Oxford, 1946-1970,
Chevalier de la Légion d'Honneur

The Danbury Press
a division of Grolier Enterprises Inc.

Publisher
ROBERT B. CLARKE

Library of Congress Catalog Card No. 72 85614

Printed in Italy by
Arnoldo Mondadori Editore, Verona

STAFF CREDITS
Editorial Director **Tom Stacey**

Picture Director **Alexander Low**
Executive Editor **Katherine Ivens**
Art Director **Tom Deas**
Assistant Editor **Elisabeth Meakin**
Project Co-ordinator **Anne Harrison**
Research **Cheryl Moyer**

Specialist Picture Research/**Charlotte Odgers**
Picture Research **Claire Baines/Elly Beintema/ Jeanne Griffiths/Carolyn Keay/Diana Eggitt**
Editorial Assistants **Richard Carlisle/Rosamund Ellis/ Mira Bar-Hillel/Susan Rutherford/Pamela Tubby**
Editorial Secretary **Caroline Silverman**
Design Assistants **Susan Forster/ Venetia Greville-Bell/Richard Kelly**
Illustrations **Arka Graphics/Ron McTrusty**

Production **Roger Multon**
Production Editor **Vanessa Charles**

The publishers gratefully acknowledge help from the following organizations:
Royal Anthropological Institute, London
Musée de l'Homme, Paris
International African Institute, London
British Museum, London
Royal Geographical Society, London
Scott Polar Research Institute, Cambridge
Royal Asiatic Society, London
Royal Central Asian Society, London
Pitt-Rivers Museum, Oxford
Horniman Museum, London
Institute of Latin American Studies, London

PICTURE CREDITS
Cover: N.A.S.A. From Black Star, New York: **D. Moore** 52 tr. **John Bulmer:** 59. From Camera Press: **A. Schatz** 48-49. From Woodfin Camp: **D. Lorton** 55. **East Grinstead Light Hovercraft Company** 47 br. From Susan Griggs: **M. Boys** 70 tl & bl; **M. St. Maur Sheil** 42 tl. From Robert Harding Assocs: **R. Hanbury-Tenison** 63 br. **Ken Heyman** 84-85. From the John Hillelson Agency: **G. Gerster** 40-41, 72-73, 78 tl; **T. Höpker** 37 t, 66; **H. Sochurek** 47 tl, 63 tr; **S. Szabo** 80. Gamma from the John Hillelson Agency: **D. Darr** 51; **R. Depardon** 78 tr. Magnum from the John Hillelson Agency: **B. Barbey** 53 l; **I. Berry** 39; **C. Capa** 54 r; **B. Glinn** 58; **E. Hartmann** 34-35, 78 br, 84 cl & bl; **J. Nance** 62 t. **Photo Research International** 47 tr. Time Inc. from Colorific: **R. Crane** 77 tr; **F. Goro** 64-65; **R. Morse** 67 b; **R. Peterson** 44; **S. Wayman** 74-75, 77b. From Transworld: 3 r, 42 bl, 67 tl & tr; **L. Choplin** 70 tr, 71 br; **I. Cook** 57; **M. Herron** 69; **F. Kaplan** 68. **U.S. Coast and Geodetic Survey** 37b.
Key: t=top, b=bottom, c=center, r=right, l=left

Acknowledgements:
R. Buckminster Fuller, World Resources Inventory; National History Museum, London; Institute for the Study of Drug Dependence, London; Japanese Embassy, London; American Embassy, London; *The Ecologist*; Victoria Trollope; Robin Dunipace; Kenneth Gatland.

Peoples of the Earth, volumes one to twenty

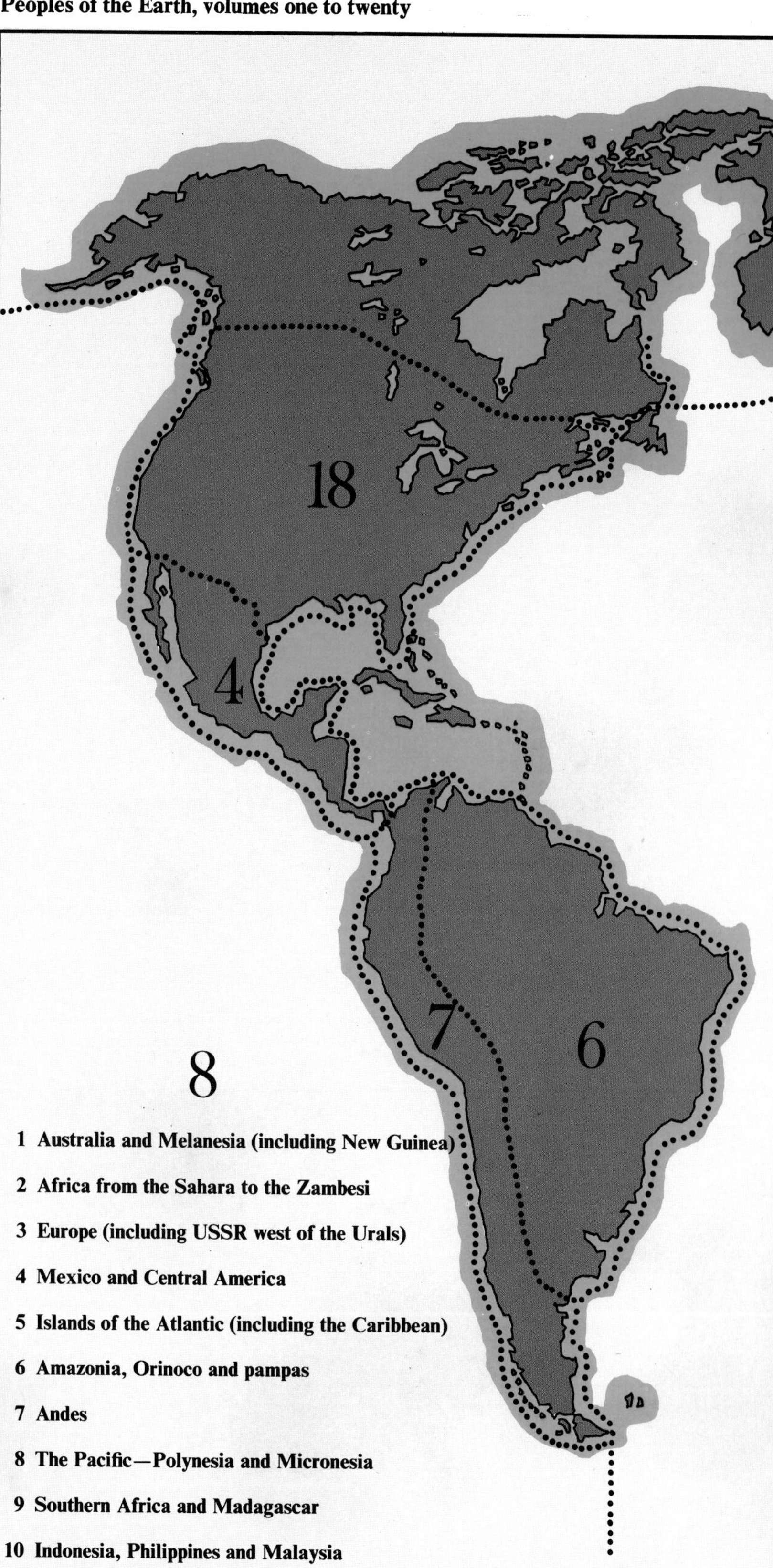

1 Australia and Melanesia (including New Guinea)
2 Africa from the Sahara to the Zambesi
3 Europe (including USSR west of the Urals)
4 Mexico and Central America
5 Islands of the Atlantic (including the Caribbean)
6 Amazonia, Orinoco and pampas
7 Andes
8 The Pacific—Polynesia and Micronesia
9 Southern Africa and Madagascar
10 Indonesia, Philippines and Malaysia

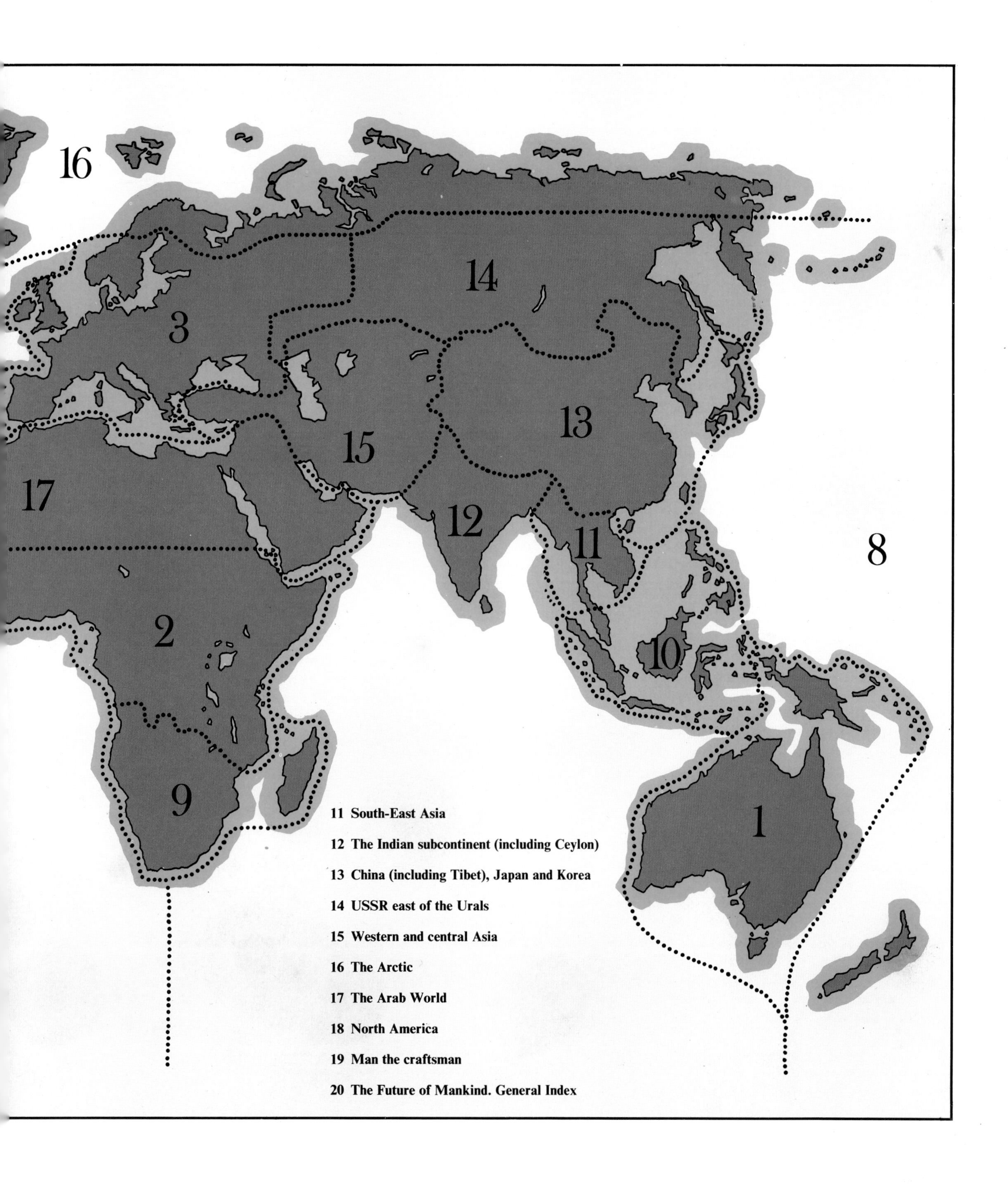

16
14
3
13
15
17
12
11
8
10
2
9
1
11 South-East Asia
12 The Indian subcontinent (including Ceylon)
13 China (including Tibet), Japan and Korea
14 USSR east of the Urals
15 Western and central Asia
16 The Arctic
17 The Arab World
18 North America
19 Man the craftsman
20 The Future of Mankind. General Index

Preface

In this series of books there have been brought together examples of human society and behavior and attitude unequalled in range and number. First published in the 1970s, the series records the world from which much of the apparent variety is disappearing – and where this variety is not actually disappearing, the uniqueness of attitude that first produced it is being subtly or rudely displaced. Take, for instance, a tribal dance that still today symbolises the myth of creation to a people for whom belief in their locally and intimately evolved myths is essential to their sense of identity. Tomorrow such a dance may receive the patronage of the state's Department of Culture and become a part of a dance repertoire for international entertainment. Such people will have been left to make do with such beliefs as they can borrow from the general pool and at best color them with local 'tradition'.

The changes today overtaking mankind are unprecedented in true fundamental respects. Hitherto, human society has produced cultures in great variety – cultures, or ways of life, that have flourished among big groups and small, and have evolved in one direction or another, sometimes influencing or overwhelming one another, sometimes faltering and dying away of their own accord. Numerous factors have contributed to them – the experience and history of the group, climate, the environment in all its aspects, the innate genius of the people themselves or of individuals among them. Each group has hitherto found its own solutions to the challenges of survival and the mysteries of existence. Sometimes a single culture has achieved dominance over a wide area for a long period – for example, that of the ancient Romans. Yet always, hitherto, the nuclei of contrasting cultures has represented innumerable, self-efficient solutions for mankind in all his variety; and where sometimes one culture has risen to great power and influence, other cultures have continued to exist elsewhere in the world, sometimes waiting themselves for the chance to impose their own ways and styles on their neighbors and so to replenish the broad stream of human history.

In our own era, however, for the first time in history, a culture has evolved that is well on the way to becoming world-dominant, allowing for no significant self-sustaining alternative anywhere on the face of the globe. The rapidly spreading technocracy of today had its seeds in the scientific approach of the ancient Greeks, an approach not resumed until the afflatus of inquiry in western Europe over 2,000 years later in the 16th and 17th centuries. It was a so-called Industrial Revolution in Britain in the 18th and 19th centuries, however, that set the new technocracy inexorably under way; and the immense inventive and economic energy of the United States and Japan in the 20th century has helped to establish the authority of the machine across the face of the globe in almost every department of human life. The fact that a third of humankind is governed by a Marxist system as distinct from a purportedly free enterprize system is of no consequence here. The technocracy – the rule of the scientific technique and its products – is with us, and with us all.

What are the consequences for mankind of the next few generations of this unprecedented change – the world-wide aspect of the prevailing technocracy? One is that more and more people will become increasingly *dependent* of its operation. Another is, surely, a growing complexification of its processes; and with this, more and more centralization. Conformity and uniformity in all but the details of life will grow more and more obligatory for no profounder reason than ease of running the system within the political framework.

The second unprecedented fundamental change that our own era has brought about in human society is the reversal of the traditional balance between country dwellers and city dwellers (in those dominant societies where cities are characteristic). A ratio, prevailing in the western world and China for millennia, 80 or 90 per cent country dwellers to 20 or 10 per cent city dwellers, has been decisively reversed in the last handful of generations – a trend now overtaking Latin America and much of Asia. Africa will follow suit.

Here the spiritual or psychological consequences are what we must consider for man of the coming few generations. In the million or so years in which anything recognizable as human society has existed, mankind has lived and worked in close intimacy with the world of nature – with its animal and vegetable products, with its mineral offerings, with its seasons and many natural hazards and demands. This intimacy with nature has of course conditioned the evolving personality of man. The equivalent role of the city in contributing to the foundations of the human personality has been negligible. Hitherto, although civilizations have grown around cities, the cities themselves have seldom exceeded a few hundred thousand souls (many famous cities have contained much less); they have existed in obvious and daily reliance upon the surrounding countryside. Put in another way, it is arguable that mankind's association with nature is essential to the harmony of his social existence and the serenity of his individual existence.

In this series it is not our function to consider in any detail the more distant future of mankind. In this last volume of the series we seek only to extrapolate the trends in human society which we see most vividly today up to that point where they can be predicted with some surety. Were we to look further, certain other major factors would have to be borne centrally in mind, such as the consequences of interfering with the process by which the survival of the fittest has been ensured through natural selection. The future of man is, indeed, full of warnings. Yet it must also be said that mankind, having discovered the glory of creation and his own role in it, and having recorded that discovery, seems unlikely to allow it to be driven out.

'Java man', whose 600,000 year old remains were found in river gravels at Trinil, had a brain capacity about three quarters that of modern man.

How man began

The story of man and his ancestors is like a play in which the key character does not appear until the last scene. Yet by the time he finally makes his entrance the audience has already got a very good idea, from what has gone before, of the sort of person he is going to turn out to be.

To say man is the 'key' actor in the drama of primate evolution is, of course, to take a very biased view. There is no doubt that if this article were being written by a giraffe, for example, man might find himself allotted a very minor and probably obnoxious part in the evolutionary saga of the primates. It is natural that man should be self-centered in his approach to primate evolution but that does not mean that he is incapable of thinking in any other way.

Many of my zoological colleagues, for instance, are principally interested in analyzing the background of the non-human primates, the lemurs, monkeys or apes. But I am an anthropologist which means that man is the central theme of my research so it is not surprising that I am primarily interested in the appearance of those structural and functional features by which we characterize man today. This being so we must clarify our ideas and decide just what we should be looking for in the primate fossil record.

First of all we must examine the nature of our criteria and select those characters that are unique to modern man and can truly be called his 'hallmarks'. There are quite a number of characters that we might choose, but bearing in mind that our source material is limited to fossil bones and teeth, the range is inevitably rather restricted. For example, the possession of language is the most outstanding human hallmark of all but unfortunately it leaves no trace in ancient bones.

One can make all sorts of inferences that speech evolved at such-and-such a time but there is no scrap of direct evidence to support such an assertion. The ability to speak lies, first of all, in the shape and musculature of the mouth, tongue, soft palate, pharynx and larynx; and secondly in certain areas of the cortex, or outer shell, of the brain which govern the muscular control of the various 'soft' parts mentioned above. Although many ingenious suggestions have been put forward none as far as we know can help us to recognize the capacity for speech from a study of bones, except, possibly, the presence of a high-vaulted palate, but it would be a brave but foolish man who diagnosed the capacity of language on the basis of this character alone.

There are numerous cultural phenomena which we would regard as significant hallmarks but, again, we cannot use them because they leave no anatomical evidence behind. However although behavior itself does not fossilize some of the artifacts associated with human behavior are often found at fossil sites.

Evidence of a hunting economy can be determined from the living sites (or living 'floors' as they are called) of early man. In the same way a tool-making industry can be identified. Much as a modern picnic site can reveal to an intelligent inquirer all he needs to know about the habits and social status of the picnickers, so living floors of early man with their hearths, their animal remains, their stone tools, their wall-paintings, their burials and so on can be read and interpreted. Archaeologists can build up a reasonable picture of the life-style of early man from a study of such débris. They are aided in this task by the evidence of palynology, a rapidly growing branch of archaeological science whereby fossil seeds and fruits provide valuable information about the prevailing vegetation, which in turn provides further evidence for interpreting the ecological status of ancient populations.

Unfortunately the background to man that we are committed to investigate extends many millions of years further back in time when no living floors and no artifacts existed. Apart from the evidence of stone or bone tools as supplements to our understanding of human manual dexterity and intellectual advancement we shall not be leaning very heavily on the evidence of 'fossil behavior'. What, then, are to be our criteria?

When we think about man and compare him with non-man one of the first things that strikes us is that he stands upright and walks on two legs. As a definition this is not nearly precise enough. It fails to exclude the fact that there are many non-human primates who are also capable of upright bipedalism. In fact it can be said that all primates either *sit up* with their bodies held more or less vertically, or *stand up*. Most of those primates who stand up can – under special circumstances – walk on two legs. The 'special circumstances' usually involve the need to carry food or other objects in their hands. The apes, the gorilla, the chimpanzee and the gibbon are particularly adept at bipedal walking but, it must be emphasized, bipedalism is not their normal or preferred gait; they walk on two legs to meet a specific situation just as man, in whom bipedalism is normal and preferred, occasionally resorts to swinging by his arms or crawling on all fours when some peculiar situation demands it.

For a more exact criterion we must draw upon our knowledge of the bio-mechanics of human walking. Human walking is a highly complex affair. This is not the place to stuff you with technical details like a Strasbourg goose with rich food, but to ask you to accept the simplified – but nonetheless valid – conclusion that modern man shows a unique method of walking which we refer to as striding. Striding involves the muscles and the joints of the vertebral column, the pelvis, the leg and the foot in a complicated and precisely integrated series of maneuvers. An alternative term for striding is heel-toe walking. This is best studied in terms of the foot. It should be noted that the final thrust that propels the body into the next step is executed by the big toe which, in men, is a relatively massive structure compared with other

John Napier

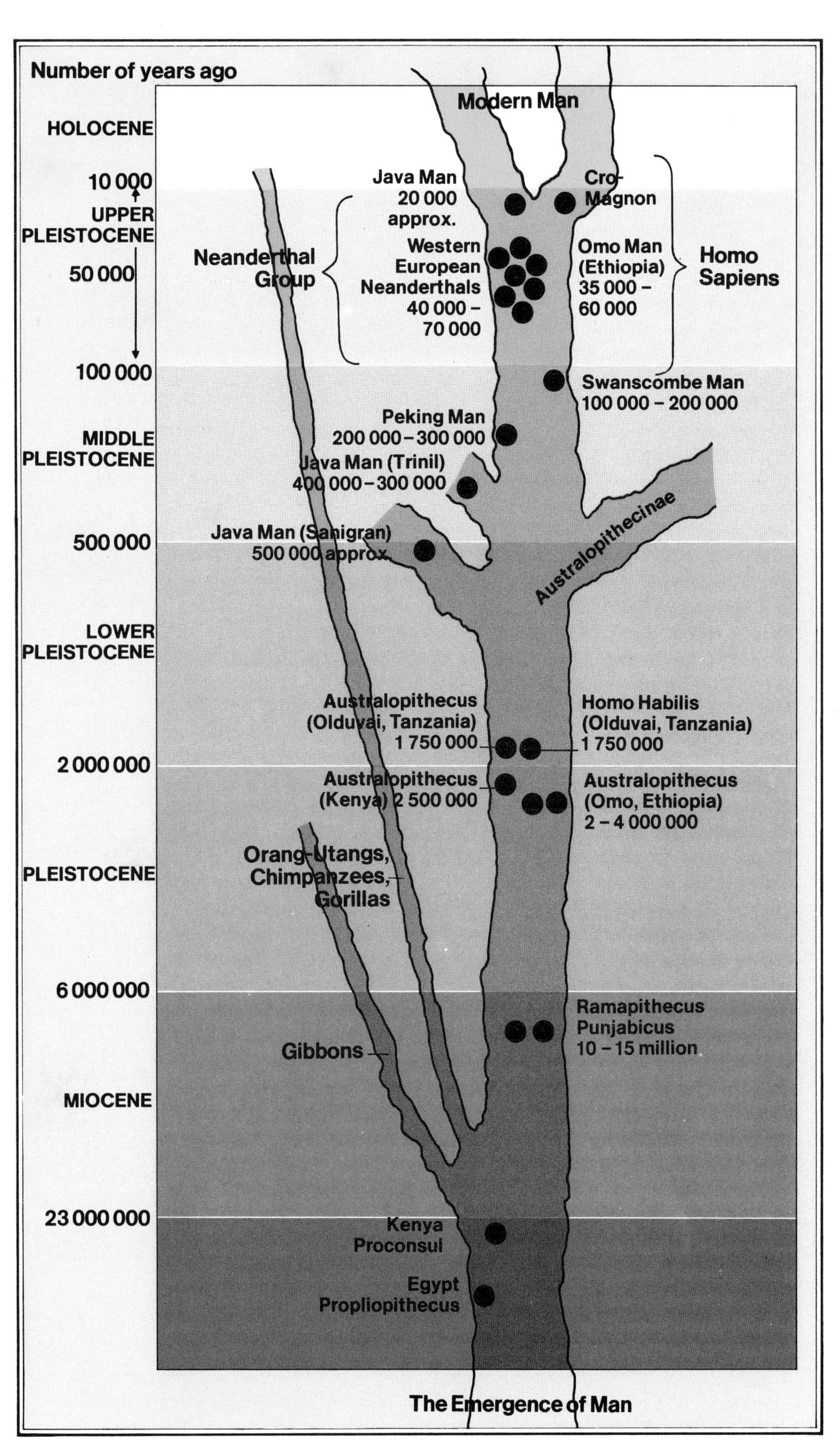

The Emergence of Man

primates. We are now in a position to formulate our first hallmark:

> man stands upright and when walking he habitually uses a bipedal, striding gait. He has a relatively massive big toe which is adduced to the other toes and not separated from them as in all other primates.

The second characteristic that strikes us is the dexterity of the human hand which is infinitely capable, exquisitely delicate but, at the same time, alarmingly powerful – powerful enough to cleave a brick in half with a karate chop, or to tear a city telephone directory into two equal parts.

The essential component of the human hand is its opposable thumb. An opposable thumb is one which is capable of being rotated about a vertical axis so that it comes to lie diametrically opposite the index finger. This anatomical characteristic provides the means for grasping objects with strength (the power grip) or with delicacy (the precision grip). The opposable thumb is therefore an obvious hallmark, but unfortunately it is not unique to man; all living old world monkeys and apes possess opposable thumbs.

Once again we must draw upon our knowledge of the functional anatomy of man's hand to set us on the right track. Man's precision grip is much more sophisticated than any monkey's or ape's; when he places his forefinger and thumb together in a precision grip he is employing the two most acutely sensitive areas in his whole body. The sensory input from these small areas of skin provides the neurological basis for the sort of skill that a watch-maker, a plastic surgeon or an assembler of micro-circuits possesses.

A few years ago, in order to provide a means of quantifying the precision grip of primates, I introduced a simple ratio called the opposability index to express the relative lengths of the forefinger and thumb. The opposability index of men is 65 which indicates that he has a long thumb.

The chimpanzee has a short thumb combined with long fingers which gives him a low opposability index (43). Functionally interpreted these two indexes reflect the differing adaptations of man and chimpanzee. Chimpanzees today are partly tree-living and partly ground-living creatures, but in the distant past they were wholly arboreal. In the trees, chimpanzees move about and feel by arm-swinging and arm-banging. Their arms are long as well as their hands and when feeding they provide a long reach for plucking fruit from shorter branches that would otherwise be out of reach. There is no great manipulative skill involved in this activity, nor do chimpanzees rely in any way on a high degree of manual dexterity for their survival. Man, on the other hand, does. His way of life is largely attributable to the skilfullness of his hands. Thus the proportions most conducive to dexterity have been the subject of strong natural selection. Now we are in a position to formulate the second hallmark:

> man possesses an opposable thumb whose length is approximately 65 per cent the length of his fore-finger.

The third feature that strikes us about man is that his brain is large and rounded; but of course brains do not fossilize and so we can only make deductions about the brain from the study of its container – the brain-box. Unfortunately, apart from overall shape and size, there is no means of determining the nature of the brain by a simple examination of fossil skulls.

What is more, size itself is a somewhat misleading indicator because it is extremely variable within a species. For example among modern human populations the brain volume ranges from 950–2,000 cubic centimeters. The average volume is about 1,350 cc.

Brain size is a valuable guide to the palaeontologist who is attempting to follow the track of man through time. From the earliest pre-human stages to the final flowering of the human family exemplified by the species *Homo sapiens,* a steady trend towards enlargement is seen. Here, then, is the basis of our third hallmark which can be expressed thus:

> man, relative to his body size, has a larger brain than any other mammal. In absolute terms it may exceed 1,350 cc in volume.

Finally, we note that man possesses small, even teeth arranged in an elegant parabolic form in his upper and lower jaw. The human teeth, like those of all living primates, are of four types: incisors, canines, premolars and molars. Together in both jaws they total 32, a number characteristic of all old world monkeys and apes but not new world monkeys and prosimians.

Unlike the apes, man's teeth are all more or less the same vertical length. The canines which form massive elongated, projecting dagger-like teeth in male apes particularly are small, short and incisor-like in man. Human molars bear low, rounded cusps in contrast to the sharp, prominent cusps of apes and monkeys. The human third molar in both jaws is often small and is frequently absent, whereas in apes the third molar is often the largest of the series.

There are many other differences but these few should be adequate for the purpose of defining the fourth hallmark as follows:

> man's teeth are small and are arranged in the jaws in a parabolic curve, the third molar being the smallest of the series; the canines are non-projecting.

With these hallmarks in mind we ought to be able to pick up the trail of man during our journey through the past. The trip will be rather like traveling by train between two cities a thousand miles apart. Most railway systems are very complicated affairs with numerous junctions, switching points, branch lines and dead-end terminals, so we have constantly to be on our guard that we do not become shunted along long-forgotten tracks that simply finish up at the end of nowhere at a pair of rusty buffers.

There is a very real danger of this happening because evolution frequently involves a form of mimicry as a result of which similar characters crop up in unrelated or distantly related forms. This phenomenon is more properly termed parallelism. We have already seen, for example, that walking on two legs is not the unique possession of man. The theory behind parellelism is that, given a similar set of environmental opportunities, animals with a common genetic inheritance will tend to evolve in a similar way.

The best example of parallelism in primate evolution is that the monkeys of the new world and the old world, which are related through a common ancestor living 40 million or so years ago, share so many physical characters that it is hard for the average person to tell them apart – even when they see them side by side in a zoo.

Man has a double heritage. His earliest ancestors were tree-living creatures well adapted to moving, feeding, mating and sleeping high above the ground in tropical forests. His later forebears were ground-livers spending their days on the forest floor or in open woodland or tropical grasslands in competition with the myriads of other ground-based mammals including the large, predatory carnivores.

These two phases are complementary. Without an arboreal background, man's ancestors could never have been successful on the ground. They possessed neither the fleetness of the impala nor the killer power of the leopards, cheetahs and lions; but early man, as a result of his arboreal background, had inherited talents which were of infinitely greater value than fleetness of foot or the ability to kill with tooth and claw.

He could run on the ground and he could climb trees; he could evade dangers by subtle maneuvers undreamed of by the instinct-dominated predators, and with his emancipated hands he could use weapons and tools to protect himself and to obtain food. Hands were far more efficient than the hooves of his ungulate competitors. Paradoxical as it may seem, man's success as a ground-living primate was entirely due to his arboreal heritage.

The earliest ancestors of the primates were among the first mammals to make their appearance. At this stage, some 60–70 million years ago, primates-to-be were small, long-nosed, ground-living animals rooting among the leaves of the forest floor for their insect food, and distinguishable only by obscure characters of the teeth and skull from the other long-nosed insectivorous creatures.

With hindsight some authorities feel they can recognize these small-sized forest floor predators even though they possessed none of the arboreal characters by which we now recognize the order. They may well be right, but to those of us interested in living primates (including man) the order effectively came into being when the primates started to live in trees. Thus we have another set of hallmarks to look out for – the hallmarks of tree-living. The observant reader will no doubt become aware that some of the hallmarks of mankind are simply extensions – refinements really – of the hallmarks of arboreality. This is to be expected in view of the statement made above that man's success as a ground-living primate was entirely due to his ancient arboreal heritage.

Among the many hallmarks that might be involved, the most outstanding (both in the sense of importance and of ease with which they can be observed) concern the eyes, the nose, the teeth, the hands, the feet, the brain and the posture.

The insectivorous ancestors of the primates whose lives were lived on the forest floor had long olfactory snouts which were adapted for rootling among the dead leaves and débris, and sensitive 'antennae' which took the form of long whiskers or vibrissae which provided the face with an acute sense of touch. Most non-primate mammals retain such vibrissae; witness for example the whiskers of a cat which do not lie on either side of the mouth but occur under the chin, in front of the ears, outer cheeks and on the brows. Higher primates, like monkeys, apes and men have transferred the tactile functions of vibrissae to the lips and to the hands. They have also reduced their snouts, and with this, their sense of smell. Primates on the whole are rather short-faced. Linked with reduction of smelling ability the eyes have taken on a much enhanced function. They have converged by migrating from the sides to the front of the face. One result of this shift is that the visual fields of each eye overlap and thus provide the basis of stereoscopic vision. The possession of three dimensional vision not only enhances an animal's agility in trees but aids in detecting prey (as in cats, owls and hawks) and in fruit and leaf plucking and hand-to-mouth feeding.

Shortening of the snout is also associated with reduction in the number of teeth and a general closing-up of the tooth rows so that contiguous teeth are in contact rather than being separated by wide gaps as they are in insectivores and carnivores for instance. The number of teeth has been reduced in primates from 44 in insectivores to 32 or 36 in monkeys and 32 in apes and man.

When early primates adopted an arboreal habitat their dietary habits changed. From a largely insectivorous diet they became more herbivorous, eating tree-products such as fruit, leaves, buds, resin and flowers. This shift required major changes in the anatomy and the function of the teeth. The molar teeth, for example, lost their piercing and slicing ability and became grinding and milling devices, and the front teeth (incisors) became broad and chisel-shaped tools for chopping and cropping. Perhaps the most far-reaching arboreal adaptation of the primates is prehensility of the hands and feet. The power to grasp by placing the thumb (or big toe) on one side of a branch and the fingers (or toes) on the other, provides an immeasurable advantage to an arboreal creature. The basis for prehensility is opposability in which the thumb (or big toe) can move independently of the fingers. In some primates it can be swung round so that the pulp surface of the thumb lies diametrically opposite the pulp surfaces of the fingers. In addition to providing a clasping mechanism for climbing and clinging, opposability supplies the basis for manipulation of objects which can be gripped between the pulpy undersurfaces of the tips of the fingers. Unlike most mammals, whose fingers and toes are topped by claws for gripping, primates have flat or flattish nails. This adaptation allows a crude claw-grip to be replaced by a much more precise manual grip.

The brain of the arboreal primates is considerably more advanced than that of living insectivores which can, with reservations, be considered as 'models' for the distant forest floor living ancestors of the primates. Primate brains tend to be bigger overall and there are differences in the size and importance of various brain elements. For example the area of the brain that interprets the functions of smell is reduced as might be expected from the changes in the olfactory mechanism discussed above. By the same score the visual areas of the brain are much enlarged. Other changes are seen in the cortex (or outer shell of the brain) and in the cerebellum which is concerned with the co-ordination of muscular activity.

Finally a discussion of arboreal hallmarks would be incomplete without reference to body posture. The striking upright stance of man – his much vaunted erectness – is not a new possession but an ancient part of his heritage. All non-human primates *sit* upright, some *stand* upright and a few *walk* upright, so it is hardly surprising that one primate – man – has adopted the upright posture habitually.

One of the earliest locomotor patterns recognized from the fossil record is called vertical clinging and leaping. This posture and locomotor complex which is first recognized in some primitive primates of the Eocene epoch (a geological period which began 55 million years ago and lasted for 18 million years) and is still to be found in certain living primates such as the tarsier, is characterized by *uprightness* of the trunk, as its descriptive name indicates. Anatomically vertical clingers show a frog-like proportion of hind and fore limbs, the ratio being approximately 2:3. A relatively recent locomotor specialization amongst primates is known as brachiation. This form of activity is typified by the gibbon, an ape which moves about the trees by arm suspension and arm swinging; once again the posture of the trunk is upright. The gibbon's limb ratio, 3:2, is the reverse of the tarsier's. Thus, in these two specialized forms of locomotion bodily uprightness is the essential feature. The majority of primates are quadrupeds. Upright sitting and occasional upright standing are the rule.

These then are the arboreal hallmarks of primates. We can now return to a rapid and rather selective survey of the primate fossil record in order to determine where and when the first evidence of the typically human hallmarks appears.

The lemur-like Eocene family, the Adapidae, which included the genera *Smilodectes* and *Notharctus* possessed most of these arboreal adaptations: nails had replaced claws and sensitive touch pads were developing on the finger tips; the eyes were converging and the snout was becoming shorter; the brain was relatively large; the legs were considerably longer than the arms and their locomotor pattern is inferred to have been of the vertical clinging and leaping variety. Other Eocene forms such as *Necrolemur* an early European tarsier-like primate, and *Hemiacodon* a North American Omonyid, are also inferred to be vertical clingers.

The next recognizable stage in the fossil record occurred during the Oligocene epoch which started 37 million years ago. At present the ancestor descendant link between Eocene and Oligocene primates has not been proved but the inferences are well-founded. Most of our information about the Oligocene primates comes from a region of Egypt called the Fayum, now desert but once covered with dense tropical swamp forest.

Between 25 and 37 million years ago the Fayum was the home of an extraordinary variety of ape and monkey-like creatures. Some, like *Parapithecus,* were probably destined to become true monkeys; some, like *Aeolopithecus,* to become 'half-apes' like the gibbons, and some, like *Aegyptopithecus,* to become true apes like the chimpanzee and the gorilla.

It has even been suggested very tentatively that one of these creatures called *Propliopithecus* represents the earliest known members of the human lineage. Both *Propliopithecus* and *Aegyptopithecus,* of which only teeth or jaws are known, show some of the characters which anticipate the human condition. *Aegyptopithecus,* has features which are strongly reminiscent of later apes and later man for that matter.

This raises an important point: the relationship of man and apes. Nearly everyone would agree that their relationship in terms of anatomical structures and physiological and biochemical functions is extremely close. The principal issue is how close? When did the ape line and the human line diverge?

There are at least four schools of thought which we can call the 'late-late', the 'late', the 'early' and the 'early-early'. Personally, I favor the 'early' school which would hold that the human lineage dates back to the Miocene epoch some 15 to 20 million years ago.

Although there is no certainty that we have identified the earliest ape-like ancestor of man, there is something to be said for the Miocene species from Kenya, East Africa called *Proconsul africanus* as a possible candidate. The gait of *Proconsul* was quadrupedal and therefore

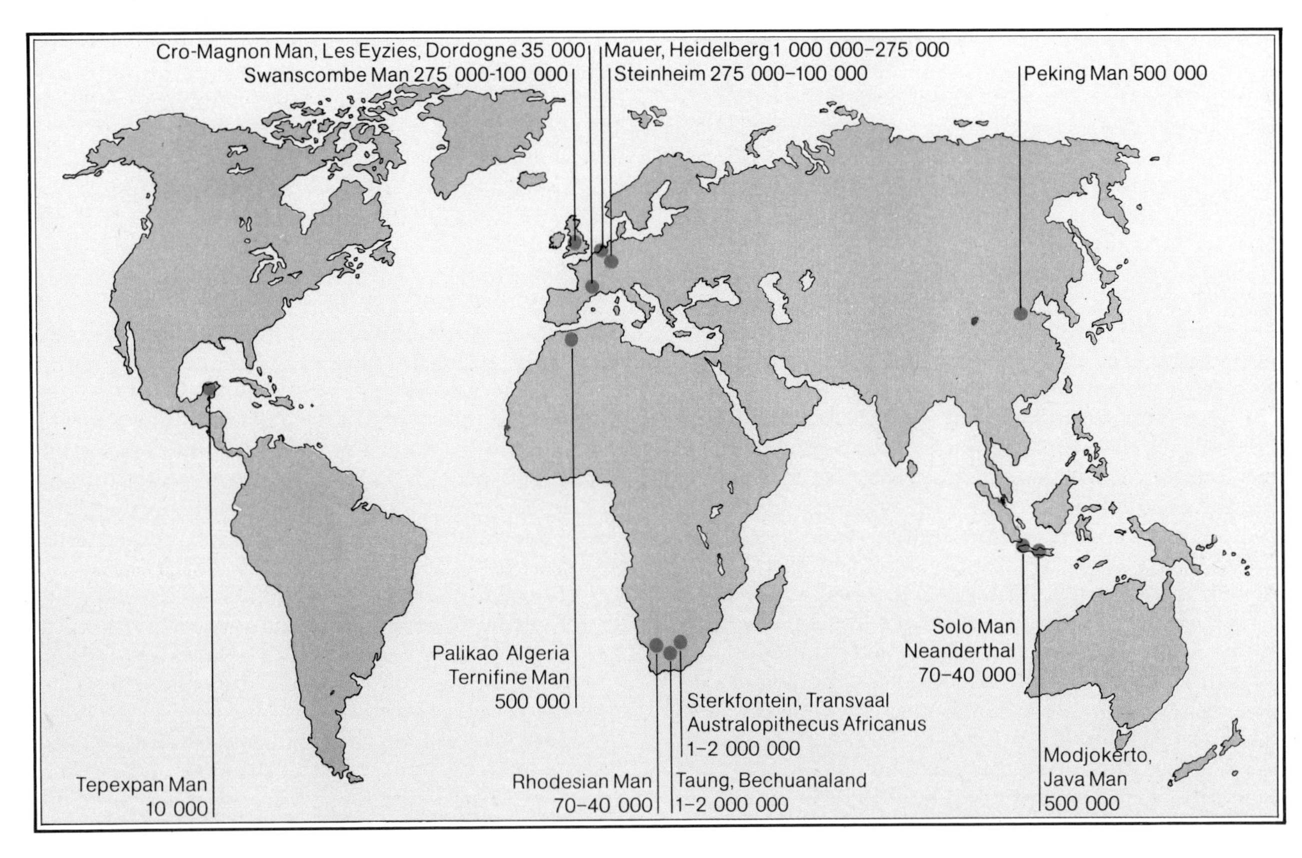

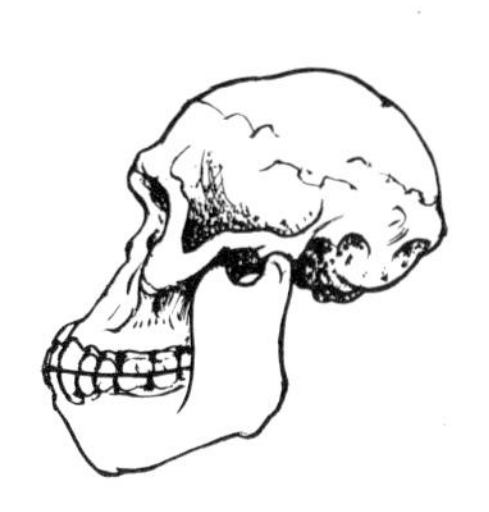
Australopithecus

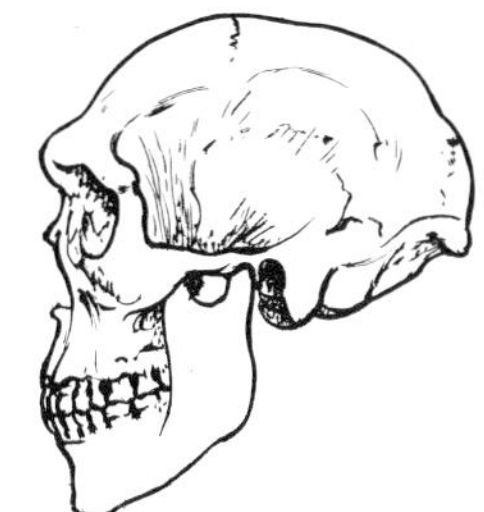
Rhodesian man

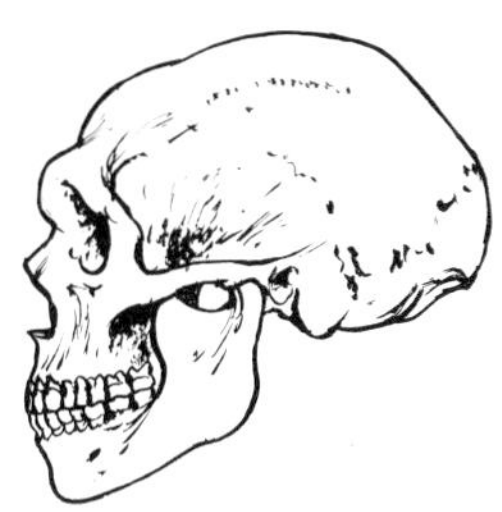
Neanderthal man

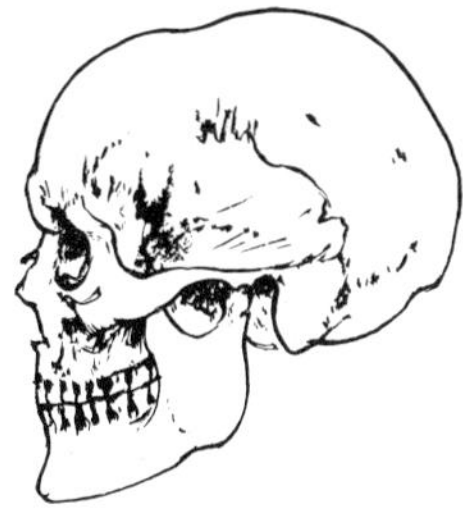
Cro Magnon man *(similar to today's long-skulled races)*

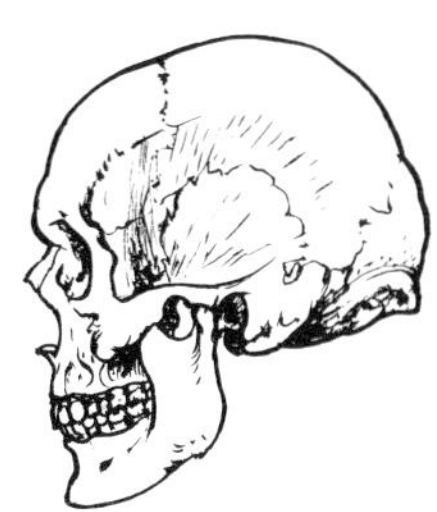
Short skulled modern man

provides no particular hint of future bipedalism. The hands are rather human-like in proportion but the evidence of an advanced type of precision grip is absent. The opposability index has been estimated at 56. The brain is still rather primitive but was quite large in terms of body-size, and the teeth – like those of *Aegyptopithecus* – are ape-like rather than man-like, but not so completely specialized that one could not envisage an evolutionary reversal to a human-like form.

During Miocene times volcanic activity, rift-valley formation and mountain-building were in full swing. One of the consequences of this orogeny and the coincidental cooling of the earth's surface, which had been steadily proceeding since the beginning of the Eocene epoch was the spread of grasslands at the expense of forests. Grasslands – or savannas – offered new evolutionary opportunities to a wide variety of mammals, including the 'over-crowded' primates in the rapidly shrinking forest zones.

A few primate stocks, including the ancestors of man and the ancestors of the modern baboons, evidently reacted swiftly to the challenge of the changing environment, and thus new horizons were opened for our remote human ancestors. The evolution of the critical hallmarks of mankind soon followed.

The earliest human ancestor as we see it at present was a creature called *Ramapithecus* from two sites, one in west India and another in East Africa between 12 and 14 million years ago. The material evidence for the potential humanity of *Ramapithecus* is slight and consists only of jaws and teeth but is, nevertheless, very revealing.

Ramapithecus has a distinctly man-like tooth form lacking all the ape-like characters seen in *Aegyptopithecus* and *Proconsul africanus*. The dental arcade is rounded, the canines are small and the molar teeth do not increase in size from front to back as they do in the apes. In the absence of any fossil bones below the neck it is not possible to make any direct conclusion regarding the posture, gait and general way of life of *Ramapithecus*. However there are several corrections between the form of the teeth and the life-style of the tooth bearers that can be adduced. For instance, it has been suggested that shortening of the canines in the transmutation of ape to man, can be closely associated with the manual use of weapons. The use of weapons, in turn, presupposes an upright posture. Similar conclusions can be made about the diet and they, in turn, can be utilized to puzzle out the sort of environment in which *Ramapithecus* lived.

The next recognizable stage in the human lineage started, apparently, at least 4–5 million years ago. There is fragmentary evidence that pre-human creatures belonging to the genus *Australopithecus* existed in two areas of East Africa, called Kanapoi and Lothagam. We pick up the trail of these near-men two million years later in the area of Lake Rudolf in northern Kenya, in South Africa, and in Tanzania at Olduvai Gorge; in all these regions they are most prolific. The early (Lothagam and Kanapoi) *Australopithecines* do not tell us very much, but the later forms in East and South Africa show many of the characteristics of the gait, brain-size and tooth form that we are searching for.

Australopithecines are generally regarded as 'near-men'. Technically, under the curious rules of current anthropology, they do not qualify for the accolade of human beings, but at Olduva Gorge 1·75 million years ago some of us accept the fact that the zoological genus *Homo* (man) first made his appearance. His way of life appears to have been that of a scavenger, a hunter of small game, and a tool-maker.

Homo habilis, as this early man is called, was a bipedal walker and probably a 'strider'; his brain was still small by modern standards but bigger than his predecessors', and his teeth showed a slight advance on the teeth of the *Australopithecines*. His hands were of a human type but lacked the refinements of precision grips possessed by modern man.

Recently a remarkable discovery has been made in East Africa by Richard Leakey. Leakey reports the discovery of a skull from East of Lake Rudolf in Kenya which has been dated at 2½ million years old. The skull is fragmented but remarkably complete. Provisional reconstructions point quite strongly to the Rudolf skull being similar to that of *Homo erectus,* with a cranial capacity of at least 800 cc. It may turn out that we have been barking up the wrong tree and that the time line to man does not pass through *Australopithecus* to *Homo habilis* to *Homo erectus*, but that the real ancestors of modern man were evolved in parallel with *Australopithecus* and *Homo habilis* and that these two genera were unproductive sidelines that eventually became extinct.

Homo habilis was succeeded in the fossil record by *Homo erectus,* known from South-east Asia (Java), Asia (Pekin), Europe (West German), and both North and East Africa. Early *Homo erectus* (from Java) had a bigger brain than Homo habilis (*Homo habilis* 656 cc; *Homo erectus* 935 cc) and the later manifestations of this species, from Pekin for example, showed a maximum brain-size of 1,225 cc.

In spite of this large brain volume *Homo erectus* possesses a skull of primitive and easily recognizable shape. His gait is assumed to have been both bipedal and striding. The form of his hands is unknown, so the only guide to the extent of his dexterity are the tools that he made. These fall broadly into the class of 'power tools', stone artifacts of simple construction designed for relatively crude purposes such as killing and skinning animals, cutting wood and pounding vegetable products. It has been shown by experiment that these 'power tools' could have been constructed and used in the absence of an advanced degree of precision grip.

Perhaps it was an increase in brain-size that stimulated the evolutionary improvement of the hand, but perhaps it was the other way about. Anyhow it seems highly probable that the complexity of the brain, the precision capabilities of the hand and the evolution of 'precision tools' were closely interlinked.

Exactly where and when *Homo erectus* passed the baton in the human relay-race to *Homo sapiens* is not known. It may have happened in different parts of the world, at different times and in different ways. There is no saying to which geographic population of early men the first prize should be awarded.

With the evolution of *Homo sapiens*, which is dated somewhere between 250,000-400,000 years ago, our railway journey is almost at an end and we are entering the suburbs of the metropolis. Most of us can begin to put on our overcoats and lift our cases down from the rack. The engine-driver has read the signals correctly, the signalman has done his job and our work is virtually over – over for some, but not for all. The complexities of the suburban system are still to be negotiated, and for certain anthropologists this part of the trip is a matter of deep concern.

They are the specialists in the growth of agriculture, of citizenship, of social and political systems, of the spread of populations and the intermingling of genes, processes which are leading us slowly but inexorably towards the eventual unification of mankind in a single biological and cultural entity. Only when the train comes to a final stop at the terminus – at some future date – will these experts reach for their overcoats and suitcases and dismount.

Races of man

Jack Conrad

For as long as man has been human, it appears that he has been very much concerned with differences between himself and others. A great many such differences are real; they can be seen or smelled or heard. Others, while not physically 'there', are equally real to the person who imagines them. When we speak of a particular race, most of us probably combine some real and some imagined differences in our appraisal. Also we tend to rank races in our own minds and have definite opinions as to who is highest and lowest. Man has been doing this for a very long time and gives little indication that he has tired of the exercise.

From paintings in the royal tombs of Biban al-Muluk (Valley of the Kings) we know that ancient Egyptians differentiated four racial groups on the basis of skin color: red, black, yellow and white. One depiction is of a red-skinned Egyptian at the head of a procession before the god Horus. He is followed in turn by a negro, then by an Asiatic and finally by a white-skinned, blue-eyed, tattooed European. It is assumed that relative closeness to the god indicates the comparative regard in which each race was held by the Egyptians. A number of other peoples have also ranked the white man last on their list of races. According to the Eskimo, for example, the Great Being tried his hand at man-making twice. His first attempt was a failure and resulted in an inferior creature called *kob-lu-na* or 'white man'. Profiting from this unsuccessful trial run, he then created a perfect man called *in-nu* who of course was ancestor to the Eskimo. The Iroquois believed that the Great Spirit needed three trials before he finally created the perfect man, that is the red man. His initial efforts were wasted in producing the 'very imperfect and ill-tempered' white man and the somewhat better but still imperfect black man.

Historians of the third century BC Han dynasty described caucasians as looking 'just like the apes from whom they are descended'. A standard Chipewyan Indian expression for describing foolish behavior was 'as stupid as a white man'. A Moorish scholar in 11th century Toledo made a similar observation. 'Races north of the Pyrenees are of cold temperament and never reach maturity; they are of great stature and of a white color. But they lack all sharpness of wit and penetration of intellect.'

If members of other races have expressed their low opinion of the white man, he has had no hesitation in returning the insults. In about 1500 BC, a white-skinned Indo-European speaking people (usually termed Aryans) conquered a far more highly developed culture of the Indus Valley in India. The Aryans described their more advanced but dark-skinned adversaries as looking like apes and barking like dogs. Historians see this attitude as an early step in the lengthy development of the Indian caste system, where even now virtually all Sudra or low caste persons have dark skin.

Other examples of the white man's superior attitude toward other races are numerous. Records of early Spanish reactions to the Indians of the West Indies are replete with statements such as these: 'They've no notion of justice; they go about naked. The Indian is better off as a slave, among men, than as an animal on his own.' Later, in mid-19th-century America, the writer William Simms commented that 'Slavery has elevated the Negro from savagery. The black man's finer traits of fidelity and docility are encouraged in his servile position.'

And so the story has repeated itself for century after century. Men have looked at their fellow men, have observed differences in appearances and behavior, and for the most part have interpreted them as signs of inferiority. Lack of technological progress by a particular society has been confused with lack of intellect. Fertility rites and lack of clothing have been subjected to evaluation by a Victorian scale, and people have been judged savage and amoral in heart and mind, or at best simple children. All these ideas, this potpourri of observable fact and guesswork, have come to be associated with race, with the presence or absence of skin coloring in man. Because of these beliefs, great injustices have been done to millions of human beings. Beating, mutilation, rape, the slaughter of infants, all have been commonplace in the history of man because of real and imagined racial differences.

Few societies in the world still condone the ruthless exploitation of other peoples. Yet many racial myths live on. People of any contemporary race will have heard or used expressions such as 'They are not as human as we are.' 'You can't trust them.' 'They are naturally lazy.' 'They are still savages underneath.' 'They don't have as much intelligence as we have.' 'They have no morals.' With attitudes such as these not uncommon in our time, it is important to understand the nature of race, to compare the races along various lines, and to probe the future of race and race relations from the scientific vantage point.

With so many strikingly different-appearing people in the world, it would probably never occur to the average man that there is much disagreement among professionals as to what races really are, and in fact as to whether they actually exist. Yet this is true. Compare the following statements by two highly respected anthropologists. In his book *Physical Anthropology*, John Buettner-Janusch says 'Of course races exist! They exist today, and they probably existed in the Pleistocene as well. Race is a perfectly useful and valid term . . . A *race* of homo sapiens is . . . a reproductive community of individuals who share a common gene pool.' On the other hand Jean Hiernaux in his article *The Concept of Race* says 'In my opinion, to dismember mankind into races . . . requires such a distortion of facts that any usefulness disappears: on the contrary, only the harm done by such practices remains.'

Confusion is heightened when we find that even among

THE BASIC RACES OF MAN

CAUCASOID

The caucasoid race is represented by a Mediterranean from Spain, a northern Indian type and a northern European from England.

CONGOID

The congoids are a sub-division of the negroid race. They are represented by a pygmy from the tropical forests of central Africa and a Mende from west Africa.

CAPOID

The capoids are the other major sub-division of the negroids. There are few left. This one is a Hottentot from South Africa.

AUSTRALOID

The australoids are comparatively few in number but are found over a wide area. They are represented by a Vedda from Ceylon, a Negrito from the jungles of Malaya and an Australian Aborigine.

MONGOLOID

The mongoloids have migrated extensively in the past. The main groups are represented here by an Eskimo from the Arctic, a Tungusian from northern Siberia and a Machiguenga Indian from Peru. The largest group of mongoloids are the Chinese.

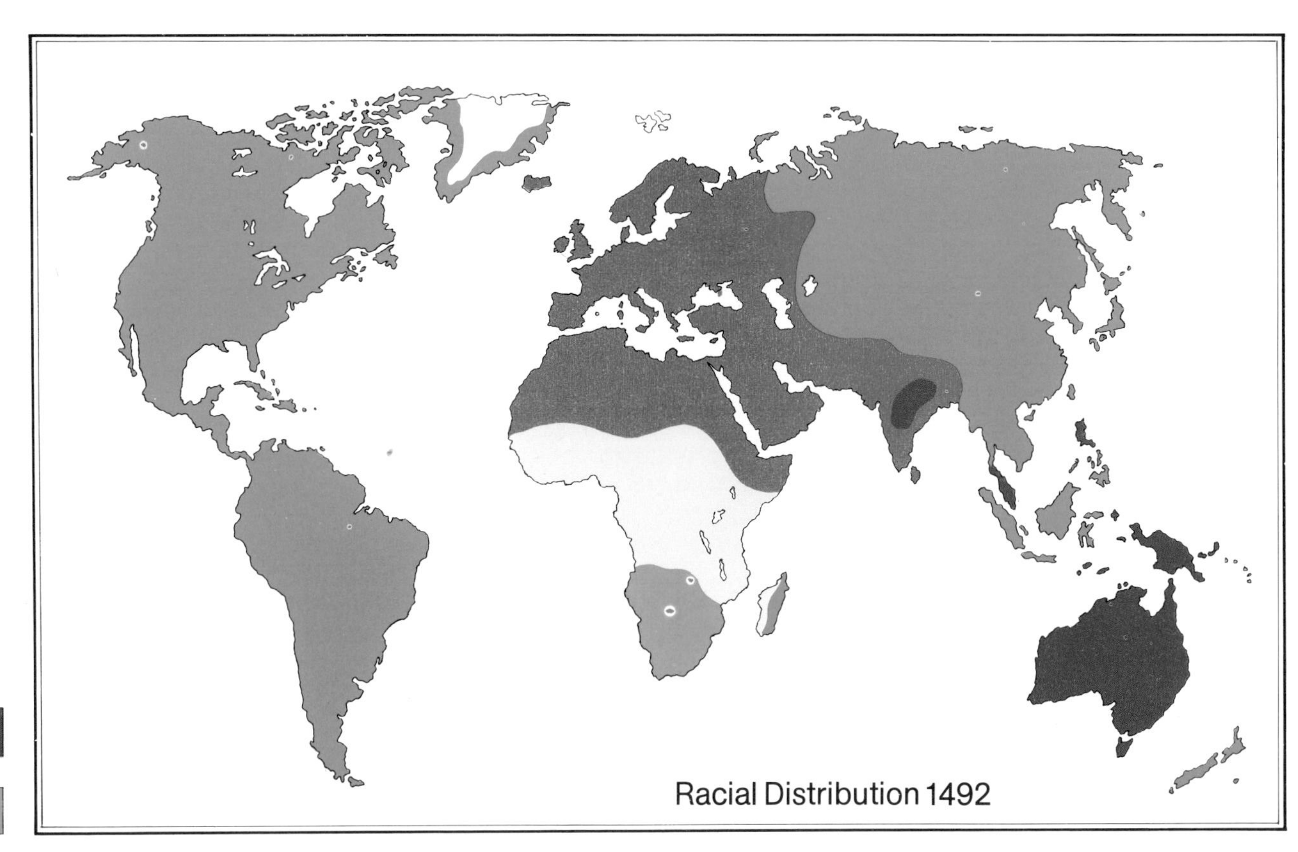

Racial Distribution 1492

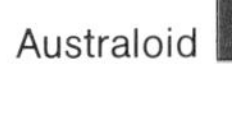

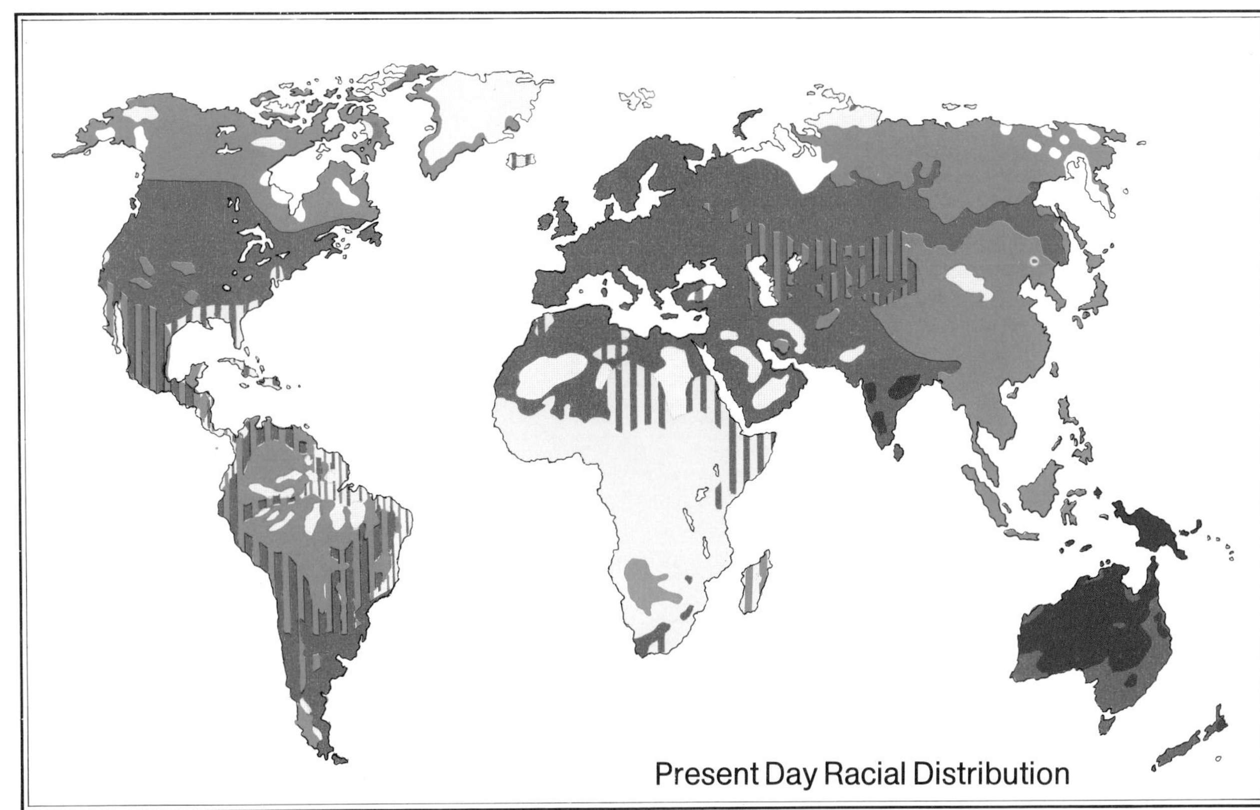

Present Day Racial Distribution

scholars who accept race as a biological reality, there is little agreement as to how they should be classified. Many use the concept of primary races, secondary or sub-races, and composite races. In such a system four grand or primary races are usually included: negroid, caucasoid, mongoloid, and australoid. Each of these is further divided into sub-races, there being for example four types of caucasoids: nordics, alpines, mediterraneans, and armenoids. Composite races are seen as the result of prolonged fusion between members of different primary races. Another system of classification argues that the negroid race is actually two primary races, the capoid and the congoid. Still another scheme lists nine geographical races, thirty three local races, and nine genetical races. Since so much disagreement does exist among professional anthropologists and biologists in this area, it is understandable that many have thrown up their hands and wished to discard the concept of race altogether.

But to deny the existence of races is to deny the empirical evidence of our senses, and the average man all over the world is not prepared to do this. Measurable and often startling differences do exist between communities of individuals who share a common gene pool. How these differences should be classified and catalogued is another matter entirely. Just as in all other areas of nature where man attempts final and all-inclusive classifications, he can only do his best, knowing that he may never understand the entire scheme of things, and that new discovery will inevitably modify whatever system he has devised.

To a large extent, the traits that are generally used to differentiate races are the obvious, the visible, the physical qualities that characterize large groups of people such as skin and eye color, the color, texture and quantity of hair, facial features, and body build. With so many observable anatomical differences, we can be certain that a great many less obvious internal and genetic differences between races also exist. This is what has confused man for so long. He sees external racial differences and surmises internal and behavioral differences as well. Unfortunately his common sense deductions about the nature of these differences are generally wrong, since as we have seen he usually confuses culturally learned behavior with innate racial tendencies.

So that we can better understand the significance of racial variations, whether superficial or otherwise, let us briefly explore some of the factors that led to the development of races in the first place. First it is clear that many racial qualities represent man's biological adaptation to the physical environment of solar radiation, climate, altitude and diet. Through mutation and natural selection human populations were able to adjust physically to a great variety of environmental conditions long before they were intellectually capable of shielding themselves through cultural innovation.

Other racial differences result from small segments of a larger population having become isolated from one another, so that the entire genetic potential of the larger group was not present for each of the smaller group. As long as they remained isolated they could not reproduce all the original genetic possibilities of their kind. Through the more intensive inbreeding that was made necessary by their small numbers certain traits became exaggerated. Still other racial differences are the result of social and cultural selection, wherein the bravest or strongest or richest or most beautiful or smartest (as defined by the specific society) mated earliest or more often, or with more members of the opposite sex, and passed on more socially advantageous genes to more offspring. The human biological variations that distinguish races are due to a variety of factors. We may now ask: if racial variation represents man's differential adaptation to his environment, his fortuitous separations from others of his kind, and the socially selective breeding dictated by the customs and mores of his group, have not all of these factors, through an immense expanse of time, conspired to produce superior and inferior races? To answer this, we need to consider three broad areas of racial comparisons, biological comparison, comparison of intelligence, and comparison of character.

Since many racial differences represent biological adaptations to climatic conditions, it follows that no one race can possibly have a body superior for all environments. The dark, tough skin of the negro is demonstrably an asset in Africa and Melanesia since it provides protection from ultraviolet penetration and insect bites. Negroes in Scandinavia, however, require Vitamin D supplements. Light-skinned caucasoids have little difficulty in the geographical north, but must continually use hats, sun creams, and insect repellents in the tropics. The long negroid forearm provides the negro with an efficient means of cooling in intense African heat and with an all-important edge in boxing. But these same long, fat-free extremities give only little protection from the cold. If we consider racial vitality or resistance to disease an index to racial superiority, we are confronted with a similar situation. In the United States, for example, it has been shown that vulnerability to certain illnesses has an almost certain racial basis. Diseases such as diptheria, hemophilia, angina pectoris, and peptic ulcer appears to be racially linked to the white race, while sickle-cell anemia, fibroids in the womb, nephritis, and hypertension have a much higher incidence among negroes. It can be seen that there are both physical assets and liabilities inherent in belonging to a race. The races are obviously not the same, but who can measure the relative superiority of angina pectoris to hypertension?

Probably the most controversial of all race comparisons deal with brains, learning, and intelligence. Many people have once and for all decided that the white race is vastly ahead of all others in intelligence and that is that. On the other hand, some racial-equality enthusiasts are just as certain, but with no more real evidence to go on, that there could not possibly be racial differences in intelligence potentials. Neither position is scientifically defensible. The plain fact is that at present we are neither able to confirm nor to deny the existence of an intellectually superior race.

Much is made of the fact that the brain size of the negro seems to run about 100 cc smaller than that of the white man. Some, of course, believe this to indicate less intelligence in the negro. On the other hand, the average Eskimo brain is about 100 cc larger than that of the average white man. We can argue that brain volume equals intelligence only if we are willing to admit that the white man is mentally inferior to the arctic mongoloid. Even within a given racial group there is a fair amount of variation in brain size, and there is no evidence that the genius has a consistently larger or smaller brain than the idiot. It appears that the richness and complexity of the neuron network within the brain is vastly more important than sheer brain size in determining intelligence.

Unfortunately there is no existing test which can determine the basic intelligence of persons reared under different cultural conditions. This is to say that, at present, innate intelligence cannot be measured without at the same time testing to some extent the opportunities and background of the person concerned. There are a host of factors that have thus far prevented the development of such a test. In the first place psychologists now speak of a variety of intelligences – verbal, mathematical, spatial, etc – within an individual rather than a single all-encompassing quality. Specific tests are necessary to measure each of these dimensions if judgements are to be made, and to construct them so that they truly measure the verbal or spatial potential of a Hottentot or a New Caledonian is a formidable if not impossible task.

Every society responds to certain aspects of its environment, but either rejects or fails to sense other features. This blindness to various aspects of reality is not found within any specific race. It is a matter of learning and often simply indicates that certain aspects of the world are of no real importance to the way of life of the group concerned. If we take our test out of the society for which it was made and use it in a society with a different set of values, sensitivities to things, and word-meanings, it seems obvious that any results we get will be worthless. If the test requires colors to be grouped, we learn that different societies group them in different ways, all equally good but not amenable to intercultural testing. If objects are to be arranged or related, the same problem arises. Tests of synonyms or vocabulary richness are also of limited value since each society builds its words around those areas of reality that are most important to it, not to others. Test items that deal with mathematics or aspects of time encounter another variety of difficulties, since there are no universal ways of conceiving of space, quantities in space, or of events in space, that is, time.

It should be recognized that if and when we are able to test adequately, racial differences in intelligence may well be found. The same may be true for specific aptitudes, temperament differences, creative potentials, and so on. The important thing to remember, however, is that even without tests it appears certain that the average member of any race is intellectually competent to live in modern society. He can be taught any profession, learn to enjoy art, literature and music, speak other languages, and maintain his behavior on a high ethical plane. Already scientists have agreed that inborn predispositions toward vices and virtues do not exist. Traits such as greediness, industry, laziness, sadism are clearly learned, not racially inherited. Character is learned rather than inherited; otherwise there would be no errant sons of model ministers. Aggressiveness, sociability, moral laxity and all the rest are products of society not of race.

In the modern world every race has its share of biological assets and liabilities. Yet as man has used his intelligence these qualities have been of increasingly less consequence in terms of survival. Most of the diseases that are linked to race have been, or are now being, erased by medication, nutrition and surgery. Man also has the future potential to erase other racial liabilities that have a social background built upon his misinterpretation and distrust of biological difference. With his mind he is capable of understanding racial difference and his own fearful reaction to it. More than this he can, and I think will in the long term, remove the social conditions which produce undesirable behavior that is often linked with race. If he persists in this, then I think the day can come when he will value a member of a different race as he does a different diamond or a different rose.

Man's early migrations

To see why and how the continents of the world are populated as they are today we must draw on the evidence of archaeology. Most of the continents were populated in prehistoric times – before the beginning of recorded history. The conclusions that we can draw are therefore conjectural rather than conclusive. The time-span involved in studying prehistory is enormous. The American continent, for instance, is probably the most recently populated part of the earth. It probably began to be peopled only about 20,000 years ago whereas a conventional date for the first appearance of man in Europe is set at 500,000 years ago.

As the art of writing appeared at different times in different places, the prehistorical period of one continent might be many years apart from the prehistorical period of another continent. The prehistoric Bantu migrations – by which the whole of sub-Saharan Africa was populated – occurred at a time when history was already being recorded in Europe, during the first millennium AD. The continents then were populated as they are today at vastly different times in prehistory. The gap between when the Amerindians came into America and when the Bantu spread over Africa was about 19,000 years. Probably the most significant population migration of the world's recorded history has been the movement of Europeans into the American continent during the last 400 years.

The human migrations which led to the world being populated as it is today started towards the end of the period of the great Ice Age – the pleistocene – which extended from about 75,000 to 10,000 years ago. Using the word migrations is in some ways confusing. The major movements of people took place over a great number of years. They were not sudden uprootings of whole populations but a steady drifting of peoples into new lands, rather like the early Saxon and Jute invasions of England which took place over centuries. Also not everyone settled in the same place. Some people went far afield, others stopped in suitable places on the way.

On a racial map of the world today one can see a jungle of different peoples. Some of them have mixed through intermarriage. Some have migrated and cast out the original population of their new home. And there are still others who remain remote from any neighbors. And if we recall that at one time negroid people lived only in Africa, caucasoid only in Europe, and so on, then the map of the world today is full of incongruities. Even 500 years ago the story was much the same. Madagascar was populated by a mixture of mongoloids and negroids; pockets of australoids are dotted in South-east Asia and Indonesia. A population map of the last Ice Age, the pleistocene, looks simpler. Then the races of man lived apart, exposed only to their own cultures in their original homes. The caucasoids are confined to the inhabitable parts of Europe and western Asia, the mongoloids to northern China, the australoids to South-east Asia, the negroids to Africa. It is from this time that we may begin to trace some of the migrations which took the people of one race into the territory of another and into hitherto uninhabited parts of the world as man spread throughout Europe and western Asia, wherever it was free of ice.

It was probably in this era that regional variations in climate and vegetation determined many of man's adaptations which we now recognize as the features of different races. In the years that neanderthal men roamed Europe men from other parts first appeared from western Asia, or from north Africa during a mild interlude, crossing the land bridges at Gibraltar and the Sicilian Straits. These were probably the earliest migrations, in response more to climatic changes than to any desire to colonize new lands, although that is in fact what happened. As the ice receded northward and forests drew across much of Europe, men flourished.

Towards the end of this Ice Age, European men were caucasoid – a general description which distinguishes them from the mongoloid or negroid races. Fifteen thousand years ago, such caucasoid men migrated back across to north Africa where their descendants today are the Berber. They also migrated east towards India where they mixed with a negroid population and evolved to become the Indians of the present day. This was the beginning of the reversal of the migrations of the people into Europe.

The rise in south-eastern Europe of the Indo-Europeans, men who tamed the horse and passed the skill on to their mongoloid neighbors in the east, changed the south to north population current to north to south, and the east to west current to west to east. Much later the Celts in south-western Germany migrated west, south and east. They were followed by the Germanic tribes and then the Slavs. Around the Mediterranean evolved the olive-skinned Europeans who migrated west to western Europe. In Armenia and Anatolia men became stockier and broader-headed and again migrated west to the mountains where they became known as the Alpine type, although they also contributed to the Russian and Slavic types. In southern Russia as steppelands appeared north of the Black Sea and the Caspian Sea a tall, fair, long-headed race evolved and migrated towards the Baltic shores. These men then acquired the distinctive characteristics of the Nordic race – fair hair, blue eyes and white skin – common even now in much of northern Europe.

The heartland of the mongoloid peoples is China and extends over regions of the world – particularly north-eastern Asia and the Americas – which were previously uninhabited. The mongoloids first emerged in China about 1 million years ago and eventually spread as far afield as the Volga river in Europe, Madagascar in Africa and Tierra del Fuego in South America.

Throughout the period of the last Ice Age it is generally believed that China was shut off from the west and its only open corridor was with South-east Asia. Then between 20,000 and 30,000 years ago, northern mongoloids migrated north-east and entered the American continent. This northerly migration was one of many, covering thousands of miles and thousands of years. The last of these was probably the Eskimo migration some 6,000 years ago.

During this Ice Age in China there were remarkably few climatic changes – the temperature decreased steadily and the land table rose. But – unlike in Europe where the glaciers moved back and forth over the millennia – in China the small changes did not foster extensive movements of people. There is one theory that suggests neanderthal men migrated deep into China from regions to the west, even before the ancestors of the American Indians departed north-eastwards. Such a movement might even explain the beaky noses and other neanderthal features of some American Indians and also of other fringe mongoloids like the Naga of the Indian subcontinent. With the present archaeological evidence, however, such a theory can neither be proved nor disproved. Another associated theory suggests that mongoloid people migrated northwards into Siberia at much the same time – 30,000 to 40,000 years ago – and by the end of this Ice Age, when the Gobi desert became impassable because of swamps, the northern mongoloids were separated from the southern mongoloids.

Until about 1000 BC the whole of the western part of central Asia as far as the Altai mountains was in the possession of 'European' tribes speaking Indo-European languages. But as the climate deteriorated, becoming colder and more arid, and as the mongoloid people were better adapted to the new climate with its cold winters and hot summers, the Indo-European tribes were forced southward and the mongoloids spread outward. The mongoloids acquired at much the same time the arts of horse-breeding and riding from the Indo-European tribes and soon became widely feared nomads. Some mongoloids attempted to overrun China – their original homeland – but most moved westward through the broad zone of desert steppelands which stretch into south-eastern Europe. First came the Huns, then the various Turkic peoples known as Tatars and lastly the Mongols under Genghis Khan.

The southern mongoloid peoples made large migrations south at a much earlier time. Yet even before their arrival in southern Asia the regions had been settled by other races like the Vedda who probably came from the west. The present population, though chiefly mongoloid, is the result of a mixture of these diverse racial elements – even including remnants of the still earlier population of australoids.

China, following the mongoloid migration from the north-west, is the center of the southern mongoloid peoples today. With its great size, however, the country is far from racially homogeneous. The north Chinese are taller than the south Chinese. In Japan too there are similar differences: people in the central rice-growing districts are distinct from those in the mountains further north. This seems to point to successive migrations to Japan, the earliest being of northern mongoloids, the later of southern mongoloids. But it leaves us with the mystery of the Ainu of northern Japan, who are often said to be the original inhabitants of the islands and ultimately of the australoid race. If this were positively established, then we could speak of an australoid migration very early on in the Ice Age which took the ancestors of the Ainu from south-east Asia north to Japan.

Australia and Tasmania were first populated by australoids. There has been much speculation about where the australoids came from, but they are generally thought to have lived in South-east Asia and Indonesia during the Ice Ages. They certainly came into northern Australia after the last Ice Age through Arnhem Land and Cape York peninsula. The gaps between the south-east islands were narrower 20,000 years ago than they are today. It is estimated that when the first Australians crossed there were only about 100 miles between Timor and northern Australia. They could therefore have quite easily drifted across. The origins of the extinct Tasmanian Aborigines still provoke argument. Certainly Tasmania was once joined to Australia and they could have settled there before the island broke away. Some think that the Tasmanians' distinctive woolly haired appearance came from an admixture with Melanesians who came from the eastern islands.

As often happens when there is a large movement of population, remnant pockets get left behind. There are various groups of dwarfed australoids, or negritos, who range over a wide area of South-east Asia. There are the small tribes of the Nilgiri hills in south India, the Vedda of Ceylon, the negritos of the Philippines, including the Aeta of Luzon and the Semang of the Malay peninsula. And possibly, as suggested above, the Ainu of Japan are a remnant australoid group.

The other early population of South-east Asia was a negroid group who got pushed out to New Guinea and Melanesia as the mongoloids started expanding southwards. The first groups entered New Guinea about 20,000 years ago and gradually continued down the crescent of the Melanesian islands. The Polynesians and Micronesians of Melanesia came much later, probably about the year 1,000 AD. They settled along the island shores pushing the ancient negroid-looking Melanesians into the mountains of the interior. Some of the Solomon islanders, for example, originated from as far away as the Gilbert and Ellice Islands, 1,000 miles to the east. In New Guinea, where archaeological studies have just begun, remains have been found which show that man certainly lived there before 10,000 BC.

The mongoloids migrated into South-east Asia later. In South-east Asia generally the main criterion regulating the migrations is not between mainland and islands but between the mountain ridges which extend like fingers southwards from Tibet and China and from the lowlands and offshore islands. The migrating populations tended to go along the valleys from north-west to south-east. The mongoloid food-gatherers gradually pushed the indigenous negroid and australoid population south and out into the islands and the antipodes, with a mixing of population on the way. The Cambodians, for example, are the most australoid-looking people in South-east Asia while the Burmese are the most mongoloid looking.

The aboriginal peoples of America are descended from Asian tribes who migrated across the Bering Strait, and perhaps also along the chain of the Aleutian Islands. The first arrived some time between 20,000 and 35,000 years ago. At that time, in the late pleistocene age, the sea level was lower than it is today for huge, expanding sheets of ice had absorbed masses of water. For the first people of this lengthy migration the continents of Asia and America were linked by an isthmus which they could cross on foot—probably unaware that they were going to another continent—just as the first settlers passed into Britain over the land that is now the English Channel. It was not until some 9,000 years ago that the continents were finally cut off from each other.

The migration of these people south from Alaska into the rest of the continent was a very gradual process. Once established in America these migrating tribes developed a character and a culture of their own. They ceased, in fact, to be Asian in any cultural sense, even though they remained ethnically mongoloid. The split with their Asian forebears was complete, probably even before the sea level had risen to fill the Bering Strait. Of these new American tribes there is no evidence that any retained traces of a distinctly Asian culture or language. And in Asia, as far as we know, none of the people retained any knowledge of the wanderers' departure, nor even wondered what had become of them. From that time on the two worlds of Asia and America were separate and oblivious of each other.

When Columbus reached America in the 15th century AD between 20,000 and 30,000 years had passed since people first entered the continent. And when, in the years that followed, the 20 million people of America were found to speak some 900 apparently different languages, America was considered linguistically the most diversified country in the world. This discovery also inspired many theories about the mixed racial origins of the American people. Only now, as we are able to relate most of these languages to one another – by placing them in a small number of large language families which are themselves ultimately related – can we be certain that this aspect of their culture is the result of thousands of years of dispersion and consequent isolation in the vastness of the continent. We may, however, accept that during the millennia there were occasional arrivals of small groups of people from across the oceans – Polynesians in north-western America, perhaps even Ainu as well. But generally we may say that the great migrations which took people to America so long ago were composed not entirely of homogeneous mongoloid tribes, but certainly of people who shared a similar ethnic make-up and a similar culture. The great differences which existed at the time of Columbus, and still exist today among the tribes of North and South America, are the result of adaptation to their local habitats.

The origins of the Eskimo are unclear. But they are a mongoloid people related to the Mongols of Asia. Man followed the retreating glaciers at the end of the last Ice Age north, across Europe and Siberia. Other groups of men moved northwards, pushed by stronger groups to the south. Throughout man's history the inhospitable northern lands have been a gigantic place of refuge. At some time, possibly about 6,000 years ago, some of the people then living in the very north-east of Siberia, distant ancestors of both the Chukchi and the Eskimo, crossed the narrow ice-covered Bering Strait to the American continent. Very probably too other groups crossed in stages, from island to island. Some of these people settled in the Aleutian Islands and, in time, developed their own culture isolated from the rest of the Eskimo race.

Gradually the Eskimo moved across the Arctic. Some groups spread through the interior of the Alaskan and Canadian Barrens, a vast inland tundra, although Eskimo have never settled south of the tree line, probably because of the threat from earlier settlers – the woodland Indian tribes. Other bands of Eskimo moved east along the coast until they reached Greenland. The northern-most living humans in the world today are the Polar Eskimo of Greenland's Thule region. Other Greenland Eskimo settled along the southern coast until the expansion of the Eskimo race was halted at what is now the Denmark Strait.

These many strands of migration continued constantly for many hundreds of years. The harsh Arctic climate has forced the Eskimo to be a nomadic people. They learnt to follow the migratory routes of the animals and fish which provide their only food. Eskimo fished and hunted on the frozen sea in winter, moved inland after game like the caribou or reindeer as they moved north in spring after wintering on the edge of the forests to the south. Migratory fish like salmon and the sea mammals – seal, whale, walrus – all moved with the seasons and were followed by Eskimo. The mammals, with their meat, bones, fur and thick layers of subcutaneous fat provided the Eskimo not only with nourishment, but also with all their material goods. The Eskimo learnt to hunt them from the sea, crossing the icy water in frail kayaks or larger umiaks. Slowly, the Eskimo settled in the most inhospitable region on earth.

The early Pacific migrations of people to the countless

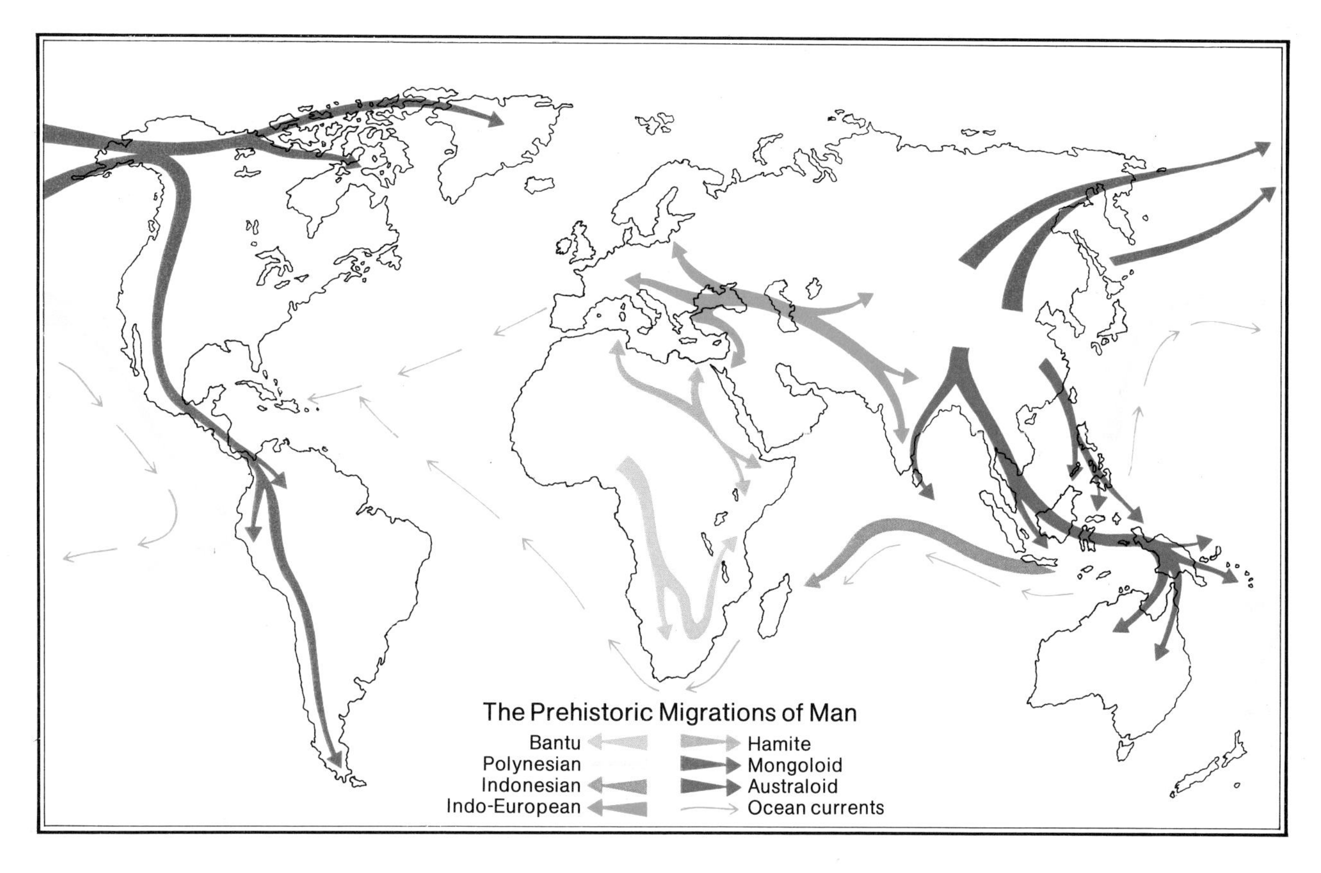

The Prehistoric Migrations of Man

islands of Polynesia have been the subject of endless speculation. Broadly, there are two theories. The first suggests that Pacific explorers set out from Asia and progressively crossed from the islands of Micronesia and Melanesia to Polynesia. To back up this theory there are many pieces of evidence, like the similarity between the Polynesian and Malayan languages, the similarity of cultural artifacts found on the islands, even the appearance of the Polynesian islanders who bear some resemblance to Micronesians and Melanesians. And if this theory is correct, then of all the Polynesian islands, Easter Island, farthest from Asia, would have had the shortest period of human occupation.

The second theory is more complicated, but employs the same pieces of evidence in a different way. There is agreement that Pacific explorers set out from Asia, heading east through the islands of Micronesia and Melanesia, settling as they went, carrying their Malayan language with them. But at some point a group split off and were carried north-west by the Japan Current – which sweeps across the Pacific from the Philippine Sea to the coast of north-west America. This would mean that Polynesians might have had a long sojourn among the islands off the north-west American coast before coming south again to settle in Hawaii, the Marquesas Islands and other parts of Polynesia. And again Easter Island, the most remote and westerly of Polynesian islands, would have been last settled. However Easter Island was in fact settled long before other Polynesian islands.

Throughout Polynesia there is as yet no archaeological evidence of any settlement before 800AD – except in Easter Island, where there was organized labor some 400 years earlier. But there has long been agreement that the first Polynesian islands were not discovered or settled by the 'Asian' seafarers until about 500AD. With the assumption that the migration went only from west to east (even if it also came from the north by way of north-west America) Easter Island could not possibly have been settled until 1500 or 1600 AD. The answer to this apparent contradiction lies in Easter Island itself. For here were built the famous giant stone statues. Their presence at last provided the key. Initially the local style of the statues strengthened the argument that they were the products of purely local imagination. But even this did not fit in with the general theory of Pacific migrations. When Europeans first arrived in 1772 the statues were already old, no-one then on the island seemed to have the skill to build others and only 100 or 200 years had passed since men had supposedly first settled there. There was, however, one other explanation and this has since been borne out by archaelogical digs.

If another people had sailed west from South America, their first stop might have been Easter Island, for it is closest to that continent. And that evidently is what happened. Excavations revealed other statues and masonry works buried beneath the ground which bore many similarities to the stone architecture of pre-Inca peoples in South America. Easter Island was the first stop for these peoples as they migrated westwards and there they built statues and other buildings. It was not until a thousand years later that the ancestors of the present population arrived, wiping out the first settlers. The statuary platforms in the Marquesas Islands are now known to have been built from about 1300 AD showing that this architectural style spread in a chronological sequence into the easternmost fringe of Polynesia.

In Africa, south of the Sahara, there are some 70 million Bantu speaking peoples. Their expansion over sub-equatorial Africa is one of the world's most recent migrations of prehistory. The main source of evidence about their origins and migratory routes is linguistic. The Bantu languages are spoken over a wide area and are very closely related to one another. Whereas the two main languages in northern Africa, Western Sudannic and Eastern Sudannic are less closely related, the 300 Bantu languages are as closely related as, for example, English and German. The Bantu languages are regarded as relatively new as the people who speak them have rapidly spread over a large area, largely replacing the older population of capoids in sub-Saharan Africa.

It seems most likely that the Bantu peoples originated somewhere in the Benue river region in the Cameroons and eastern Nigeria. They probably did not speak Bantu at all but a form of Western Sudannic. Some time just prior to the first century AD they began moving southwards into the Congo forest, possibly because of population pressures in their homeland. In any case they emerged south of the Congo forest onto the lightly wooded savanna country that was similar to the country left behind them in the Benue area. It is now known as the Katanga area of Zaïre. The climate is neither very dry nor very humid with a rainfall of about 20–30 inches a year. Here there were rich iron and copper deposits. The migrating Bantu probably knew how to work iron and copper. Certainly the Nok culture, just north of the middle Benue, knew how to smelt iron by about 250 BC. The earliest iron age date for any part of Africa south of the equator is that from the Machili Forest Station in eastern Barotseland which has been placed at the end of the first century AD. These first pre-Bantu migrators probably stayed for a long time in the Katanga area before suddenly spreading all over southern Africa. The first stage of expansion was doubtless from this central Katanga region to the coast on each side. They had a superior iron technology to the surrounding pygmies, iron weapons and tools. Their knowledge of cereal growing enabled them to take over the East African varieties of sorghum and millets introduced by the neolithic Kushites further north. From the *Geography* of Ptolemy, which is generally regarded as a work of the 4th century AD we hear of 'man-eating Ethiopians' who lived still further to the south, perhaps around Cape Delgado. This may well have been the first documentary record of the Bantu.

The explosion of the Bantu over so much of sub-Saharan Africa probably took place during the first half of the present millennium. The reasons for this sudden and rapid population expansion is probably to be found in the import of foodstuffs. We know that about 1,000 AD some Indonesians crossed the Indian Ocean on the sea currents. They came in simple outrigger canoes bringing with them South-east Asian food plants. These included bananas and coconuts, which eventually found their way into Africa from Madagascar. With these foodstuffs the Bantu were able to spread further north and south into the more perennially watered regions. They could occupy the mid-coastal belt and we know from Arab geographers that by the 10th century at least they had moved as far north on the coast as Juba. From about 500 AD onwards they spread further out all round. Some moved down and crossed the Zambesi; others moved back into the forest, while others moved north-east where they were halted by the downward moving neolithic people in northern Kenya, Uganda and Rwanda.

Western man's cultural evolution

The inexorable progress of culture – the sum total of man's knowledge, beliefs and skills – has been stimulated, widened and sometimes stunted throughout the ancient world and into the present century by trade, conquest and migration. Like an ambitious weed stemming out from itself, spreading over fields, roads and cities alike, never allowing its progress to be halted too long by any one object, it has permeated the history of the western world. The 'western' culture of today has, in the last 400 years, spread to all corners of the world and is the product of years of trial and error by our forefathers.

It is by no means perfect. In the 20th century, western man is for the first time seriously concerned about the survival of his species and of his world. Our forefathers rarely entertained such thoughts. Though we have seen them constantly at the side of soothsayers, astrologers and 'liver-readers', pleading for a brief glimpse of the future; though we find them pursuing one religion after another, and laying down fine and noble rules by which to live, we rarely find them pausing to question the purpose of their civilizations.

The western world owes its culture largely to the ancient civilization of the Mediterranean and the middle east. Here over the centuries men slowly mastered the invention of writing, the science of astronomy and the beginnings of medicine, harnessing the cart to the horse and using the animal as a beast of burden. Man began all of these things with little idea of their potential and with no concept of the eventual outcome. Man in his earliest beginnings wandered the earth blindly, upturning here and there with spades of curiosity small seeds of enlightenment which, though wasted then and often neglected by ignorant leaders, have germinated over the centuries into the scientific and artistic achievement of today.

There are two broad theories about the emergence of cultures. The first states that men developed in isolation; that there were in fact several origins of culture which developed independently. The other holds that man's ideas were diffused all over the world, that there were no separate inventions. The diffusionist theory is more credible today. Certainly in looking at the emergence of western culture one sees a continuous development from the earliest neoliths who first settled in North Africa. Yet there were advanced cultures in parts of the world that western man knew nothing of until their decayed ruins were discovered by the 16th century explorers; cultures like the Maya and Aztec in Middle America, the Inca in South America, cultures in the east and the medieval Sudannic cultures in Africa. Although there may have been contact in ancient times, unbeknown to us, these were not central to the emergence of today's world.

It was agriculture that urged man to settle – to retire from his dangerous, wandering and insecure life – and to take root. For by settling and working the land, man multiplied, and his implements improved. He found himself freed from the need to stalk his food, for the animals he had once followed and hunted, he now tamed and herded. He fed them when they were hungry and he lived off them. He cultivated the land he settled upon, and applied his mind to the development of his farming methods. He dug trenches for irrigation, and settled into a routine.

Many thousands of years ago he wandered in lonely groups from North Africa (so it is generally believed), and came across a land which offered him all that was necessary for permanently settling down: a favorable climate, food for both himself and his animals, a constant supply of water, and anything which he might need at any season. This was neolithic man – the searcher, roaming and wandering and eventually settling – changing from being a food gatherer to a food producer. He settled along the banks of the Nile in Egypt, and in the country between the upper waters of the Euphrates and Tigris and Persian Gulf – Mesopotamia, today known as Iraq. Neolithic man settled there roughly 9,000 years ago, probably several thousand years after the 'discovery' of agriculture by women. It is believed that women began agriculture, for while the menfolk were away hunting, the collection of seed and vegetables was probably the woman's responsibility. While he settled in ignorance of the tremendous alteration to human affairs his action was to cause, a third group of people, the primitive nomads, settled around the Mediterranean basin in the more seasonal lands of the European forests, the Arabian deserts, and pastures of central Asia. These people continued to live dangerously, mixing hunting with herding, and improving their weapons while their distant brothers improved their farming implements.

Thousands of years passed, and while on the banks of the Nile and in western Asia communities grew and progress carried man into the Bronze Age, time mysteriously replaced neolithic man with the first Egyptians and the first Sumerians. They and the primitive nomads developed in separate directions, and followed opposite courses destined to bring them into conflict.

Over a period twice that of Christ's birth to the present age the Sumerian civilization developed in Mesopotamia, in the south region of the Plain of Shinar, known as Sumer. Great controversy exists over which civilization arose first – the Egyptian, or the Sumerian. But though their beginnings cannot be dated, the two did evolve almost at the same time. They were linked by trade, and it is known that the Sumerians used the Egyptian word for wheat. Sumerian trade was in fact quite extensive, for it even reached India (most probably by land).

With the expansion of their trade and the growth of their government, the Sumerians found it necessary to invent a means of recording their business transactions. A form of picture-writing was developed, which was later succeeded by the cuneiform system of writing (from

Latin, *cuneus,* meaning 'wedge' – wedge-form writing). It consisted of a series of delicately drawn triangles grouped either together, or with one or a number of straight lines representing a syllable, or a word – a group of sounds. The Sumerian system never developed an alphabet of the letters which made up the syllables. The symbols were drawn on pieces of wet clay with an instrument made of bone and from strips split from a hard, reed-like bamboo. The end used to inscribe was triangular in shape, and that accounts for the variance in the lines, for one end is thinner than the other.

The Sumerian civilization was composed of city-kingdoms, all of which contested for leadership of Sumer. The nucleus of the Sumerian civilization was the temple. Here was a place of worship; here were store-houses and business offices surrounded and protected by a great wall – the temple enclosure. The Sumerian towns grew outwards from the temple enclosures. They were ruled over by wealthy priesthoods, and the chief priest ruled the town. The houses of all the citizens were made of sun-dried brick, and the towns were erected upon mounds, for buildings collapsed frequently, and when one fell it was leveled out and then built upon again. These mounds today are a hive of information for the prowling, searching archeologist.

The towns grew and became cities. The years between 3000 and 2900 BC saw the emergence of the city-kingdoms. They were ruled over by the city ruler – the *patesi,* who was above the priest, the official and the wealthy landowner whose slaves worked his lands and carried on trade with the small boat upon the river, and the slow caravan upon the land.

Though the *patesi's* taxes were very unfair, he was vital to the community in matters of war and irrigation. Were it not for his attention to dikes and canals, his incessant demand that they were constantly attended to, the crops would have died and the community would have starved. As for war, the city-kingdoms were always bickering, and if it was discovered that one city-kingdom was trying to steal a strip of land from another, the citizens of that particular kingdom were only too pleased to follow their *patesi* into battle.

Sumerian fought Sumerian. They charged one another on chariots – the earliest known wheeled vehicles, and one city-kingdom defeated another.

It was the city of Ur which first gained leadership of Sumer – a city situated close to the mouth of the Euphrates. Its ruler was Mes-anni-padda, and he is the earliest known king in western Asia. Mes-anni-padda's four descendants all ruled in Ur, and this line of five kings is called the First Dynasty (or family) of Ur. In turn they were defeated by their closest rival – the city of Lagash. But meanwhile, in spite of this preoccupation with war considerable advances were made in sculpture. Tombs have been unearthed at the site of Ur which boast beautiful contents that quite rival the findings of the Egyptian tombs. Works of gold have been discovered, treasures which will eternally fascinate. But though the Sumerians have left us wonderful works of art, their greatest and most advanced art was the art of war. Their history is an almost endless story of one city-kingdom warring with another. They were a religious people, but they lived in ignorance of the idea of living a good life on earth in order to achieve happiness in after-life. When a Sumerian died he was buried in the town, often in the court of a house or in a room. If a man had slaves and servants, they were slaughtered and buried with him to be of service wherever his soul happened to find itself. The Sumerians' impression of the next world was of a dim and dismal realm beneath the earth to which both good and bad were destined to go.

Parallel with the steady development of Egypt, and the rise and fall of Ur, the Semitic speaking nomads of the west continued to raid and trade with the Sumerians. They had not been able to defeat the Sumerians because of their inferior knowledge of the practice of battle, but in about 2500 BC, a great leader rose among them in a northern region of the Plain of Shinar known as Akkad. Here, many years before, Semitic tribes had seized the cities of Opis and Kish and came to be known as Akkadians. Their leader was Sargon the First. He united the Semitic speaking tribes and led them against the Sumerians, defeating them, and setting up an empire which reached from beyond the Persian Gulf in the east, to the Mediterranean in the west. His empire is known as the Sumerian Akkadian empire and it lasted for 200 years. But though Sargon conquered Sumeria he had to learn from them, for the Akkadians knew neither how to read, write nor govern. Because of this the Sumerians kept their civilization. When the Akkadians began to weaken the Sumerians were able to rise again and regain their kingdom – but it was not the world they had lost. In the two centuries that had passed there had been inter-mingling between the two races. Semites were as numerous as Sumerians, and so they were recognized as part of the unified nation of the ancient Plain of Shinar, which now for the first time gained a national name. The new nation was called Sumer and Akkad. With the kings of Sumer and Akkad under the leadership of Ur, there was a century of prosperity and advance, sadly followed by two centuries of decline. Conquests were made north-ward up the Tigris, even including Assyria. A large area of western Asia was brought under control, and there was a remarkable expansion in trade leading to the use of silver as a means of buying and selling. Trade brought about book-keeping, business, and the introduction of social customs which were seen as a proper way to live, and were eventually formulated into laws.

Ur flourished as trade won for it riches and wealth. The citizens erected a stunning tower temple, and in 1930 three kings' tombs were found which, although raided by the Elamites, were still able to speak of the wealth Ur

	NEAR EAST	EUROPE	MIDDLE EAST	ASIA	AMERICAS
Before 2000	The use of irrigation and crop cultivation heralded the early civilizations in Mesopotamia and the Nile valley. Maths was applied for the first time to the building of pyramids, and the passing of time reckoned according to Solar years.	The Agean civilization, centered on Crete, began to trade throughout the Mediterranean. Hieroglyphic writing developed.	The Dravidian civilization in India developed an ordered government, built cities and irrigated land.	The origins of ancient Chinese civilization lay in the Yellow River valley where Sage Kings were credited with the earliest development of agriculture, medicine and river conservancy.	Stone age people entered the continent of America thousands of years before, yet made few steps towards an organized civilization. The first Eskimo cultures entered North America from Siberia.
2000 BC	In Asia Minor, the advanced Anatolian civilization was based on law and order and wealth from iron-smelting. The Phoenician civilization traded and colonized as far as West Africa and Britain. The great age of Egyptian architecture and literature. Babylon flourished;	The Greek civilization rose to absorb the Aegean culture with the fall of Crete. The siege of Troy. Development of copper and bronze working.	The Aryan invasions overwhelmed the Dravidians. Aryans settled and inter-married. The beginnings of early Hindu literature.	The Yellow River civilization expanded under the Shang dynasty. Lunar calendar devised. Character writing developed and silk manufactured.	The time of possible contact with European civilization through Phoenician ships swept across the Atlantic to Central America.
1000 BC	The Assyrian empire conquered east Mediterranean lands. Carthage founded. Decline of Egypt, but architecture, science and medicine flourished. Growth of Judaism. Jerusalem destroyed and captured by Babylonians. Coins invented by Lydians in Asia Minor.	Greek city states flourished. Greeks learnt alphabet from the Phoenicians. Rome founded. Etruscan invasion of Italy. Pythagorean mathematics developed and the seeds of democracy sown in Athens.	With the growth of the Hindu religion, the caste system developed. The birth of Buddhism.	The Chou dynasty expanded as far as the Yangtse River. Irrigation works, dams and canals built, though central control was never strong. Skilful bronze, ivory and jade works. Confucious taught wisdom and good manners at the onset at the Golden Age of Philosophy.	In Central America, the Olmec civilization produced mosaics and jewels. In Mexico, the Mayan civilization developed hieroglyphic writing, a calendar, arithmetic and an expressionist art. In the Andes, maize (fundamental to later Andean cultures) was cultivated for the first time.
500 BC	The Persian empire destroyed by Alexander the Great, enabling Greek culture to expand. Alexandria founded in Egypt. Euclid – father of geometry – and Archimedes made strides in maths and physics. Old Testament written. The Jews under foreign rule.	With the decline of Greece, conquered by Rome, the Golden Age of the Roman Empire began. Caesar conquered Gaul and Britain, but was checked by Germanic tribes. With Socrates, Plato and Aristotle, modern philosophy was born.	India, except for the southern part, first united under the Mauryan dynasty. Buddhism established itself over most of India. A time of peace and reform, and missionaries sent to Syria, Ceylon and Tibet.	Confucianism became the state religion under the Ch'in and later the Han dynasties. The Great Wall of China was built to prevent invasions from the north.	Teotihuacán was the center of civilization in the valley of Mexico. Pyramids were built for the worship of the sun and moon. In the Andes, the Mochica and other artistic cultures developed, flourished and then declined.
0	The Roman empire supreme in the Near East. New Testament written. In Alexandria, Ptolemy constructed a map of the Solar System with a spherical world – around which all other planets and the sun revolved. The neo-Persian empire ruled in the east as far as the Indus.	The rapid spread of Christianity over much of Europe. The Roman empire divided into the Western and Eastern; the Western empire declines and falls. The era of great European migrations – Scandinavians, Celts, Saxons and Franks.	Hinduism emerged as a unifying force at a time of political disunity. The Gupta dynasty marked a Golden Age of literature, art and science. Sanskrit became universal literary language. Decimal system and use of zero discovered, later brought to Europe by Arabs.	Buddhism arrived in China from India. Paper first used. The central control and Mandarin class of civil servants was disrupted by Hun and Tatar invasions. Japan embraces the Buddhist faith introduced from China.	In Peru and Bolivia, a period of artistic splendour, centered for a time at Tiahuanaco. In the Yucatán, Central America, the Mayan civilization reached a peak with the growth in knowledge of arithmetic, astronomy and agriculture.
AD 100	Islam rose, the religion to be promoted and imposed by the Arab empire on much of the Near East. Mecca, where Mohammed was born, became a holy city, but Arab civilization soon centered on cities like Baghdad, Damascus and Cordova. Paper and block printing introduced from China.	The time of the Holy Roman Empire in which the Church served as guardian of culture. In the eastern Roman empire (the Byzantine civilization) Greek culture was dominated by a Roman system of government – an era of brilliant art and scholarship.	Buddhism disappeared from India but dominated the people of Ceylon, Burma, Siam (Thailand) and Java. Gupta dynasty in India crumbled as a result of Arab and Hun invasions. Evolution of smaller Hindu kingdoms.	Unity in China was re-established under the Tang dynasty. Science and art flourished again. Magnetic compass and gunpowder invented. Porcelain manufacture perfected.	In the Andes, successive cultures produced fine art but never quite recaptured the splendor of their predecessors. In Central America, the Toltec Indians took over Teotihuacán and built splendid cities.
AD 1000	The Ottoman empire rose under the Turks – a central Asian people – and came to dominate much of the old Arab empire, maintaining the faith of Islam. The Arabs eventually expelled from Spain by Christians. Turks blocked western trade with the Far East.	The Middle Ages, with the growth of European states. Christian crusades against Islam. Universities built. Separation of western and eastern Churches. Beginning of the Renaissance and the Reformation with their intellectual and artistic revolutions.	Muslim invaders from the west overran the Hindu kingdoms and began the bitter rivalry of the two faiths.	China became part of the Mongol empire for a time, until the Mongol rulers were driven out by the Ming dynasty. Kublai Khan visited by Marco Polo. In Japan, painting, architecture and landscape gardening flourished.	The rise of the Inca and Aztec civilizations in South and Central America. In both these cultures, the people worshiped the sun from their pyramids, and possessed efficient political and war systems.
AD 1500	The Ottoman empire broken up, Turkey founded, and the Arab states emerged with Arab Nationalism. Islam retained its hold over the eastern Mediterranean lands—except in Palestine where a Jewish state was founded.	The age of Reason and Exploration. The emergence of Industrialism and Socialism. European states frequently at war with each other. Science, materialism and rationalism eventually replace religion as the dominant force in European civilization.	The Mogul (Muslim) rulers dominated India until European traders began to vie for the country's wealth. The British won India to their empire, and imposed their élitist culture until India achieved a popular independence and an un-popular partition of India (Hindu) and Pakistan (Muslim).	In China the Manchus founded a new dynasty. European traders gradually made contact with the Chinese. The collapse of Imperial China was followed by the emergence of a new socialism. Japan entered an era of high industrialization and became a modern state.	The European discovery of America heralded the utter destruction of the Aztec and Inca cultures. Colonization on a large scale followed the extraction of riches. Western civilization and soon in-dustrialization initiated the rise of independent and dynamic American states.

knew at that time. There was literature, though our only knowledge of it is that which we have learnt from the school-books and exercise tablets found belonging to the pupils of that distant age. The literature consisted of stories and mythical tales, the most famous being that of the hero Gilgamesh, who failed to gain immortal life though he passed through many strange and unusual adventures. He was a popular hero whose adventures were passed on from generation to generation. The Greeks called him Hercules.

The splendor of this age of Ur was never forgotten. It represents the highest level of the Sumerian Akkadian civilization – the civilization we now call Babylonian. But shortly before 2000 BC it fell. Not only was it wrestling with wars within itself, but from the east it was attacked by a new race of people – the Elamites, and simultaneously it was invaded in the west by another Semitic tribe – the Amorites. Together they destroyed the Sumerian Akkadian empire, and they fought each other for leadership of the conquered world.

The Amorites settled in a small, obscure village by the name of Babylon. They held it for three hundred years – from roughly between 2050 to 1750 BC. In that time they made it a pinnacle of wealth and power so outstanding that its name was given to the Plain of Shinar, and was thereafter known as Babylonia.

The Elamites and Amorites continued to squabble for complete rule over the Babylonian Plain, and after a hundred years of vain fighting a king came to the Amorite throne who was to defeat the Elamites and drive them back to their home in the mountains of the east. He was Hammurabi, the sixth in the Amorite line of Babylon kings. He ruled from 1948 to 1905 BC, and devoted himself to peaceful governing, gaining for himself a place in history equal to that of Sargon the First.

Once again, another conquest brought about progress. Though one empire defeated another, advance continued. As in the time of the kings of Sumer and Akkad, trade under Hammurabi penetrated the ancient world yet further, and the slow, wandering caravans of the Babylon traders spread cuneiform writing into western Asia – into Syria, and Asia Minor, passing onto one the knowledge of another.

There were schools, learning, and a progression in the art of future-reading. Man had always been a superstitious animal, intensely interested in knowing his future, and professional soothsayers and 'liver-readers' preyed upon him like flatterers upon the rich.

There was what Hammurabi believed to be justice. Hammurabi tried to govern fairly and generously, and though he ran his empire with great vigor, judgement and confidence, his ruling of 'an eye for an eye, a tooth for a tooth' often proved unfair. If a building collapsed and killed a son for example then it was the innocent son of the builder who was killed as a punishment.

Art appears to have made little progress in Hammurabi's time. The arch began to be used more frequently at the front of buildings, but the poverty and lack of beauty of the few pieces of sculpture excavated seem to be almost a prediction of the tragedy Babylon was destined for. For Hammurabi's empire barely survived his death. In about 1750 BC, a savage people appeared from the east and northeast, and they wrecked and ruined Hammurabi's world and held it in a state of stagnation for over a thousand years. These were the Kassites, and here we see conquest stunting the growth of civilization and progress. History's poisoned needle plunged Babylon into a thousand years of sleep, to be kissed into consciousness again at the end of that period by the Chaldeans. And while it is sleeping, let us leave it and examine that other civilization on the banks of the Nile so important to the story of western culture.

Egypt's beginnings are very similar to those of Sumeria. They too, lie in agriculture. Communities settled at two points along the Nile, and these grew to be the first known nations – Lower and Upper Egypt. They were ruled over by kings and, possibly in the 43rd century BC an unknown king of Lower Egypt conquered the kingdom of Upper Egypt and united the two kingdoms. An era known as the First Union followed, and Egypt was ruled from its first capital situated mid-way between the two kingdoms – Heliopolis. It was responsible for the administration of the complex irrigation system the Egyptians had built themselves on a national level. This, as well as using oxen for plowing, increased the annual turn-over of their crops considerably.

The First Union saw the drawing up of a 365 day calendar. Years were not numbered, but referred to by the most outstanding event connected with whatever king may have been ruling. The picture writing which they had invented was followed by a phonetic writing, and which in turn progressed even further until the Egyptians drew up the first known alphabet. It contained 24 letters. Ink was made of soot and water, a pointed reed was used as a pen, and a river weed called *papyrus* was split into thin strips and used as paper. It is from the word papyrus that the English word *paper* derives.

The First Union eventually collapsed and the two kingdoms existed independently for a while. Then, in 3360 BC a second union was formed by Menes, and copper was mined. His early successors had carved upon the neighboring rocks of the mining tunnels of the Peninsula of Sinai huge records of their presence there.

Expeditions during the rule of the early Pharaohs of the Second Union sent men by sea to Byblos, on the coast of Syria, where timber was cut and brought back to Egypt for boat and house-building, and all kinds of carpentry. There was extensive trade and shipping, and the introduction of copper tools led to building with limestone rock. Until that time the Egyptians had only built with sun-dried brick. In the 30th century BC, the architect Imhotep built a beautiful stone tomb for

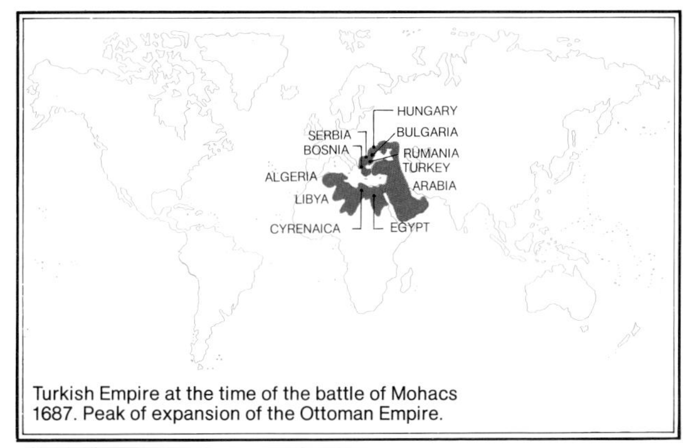

Turkish Empire at the time of the battle of Mohacs 1687. Peak of expansion of the Ottoman Empire.

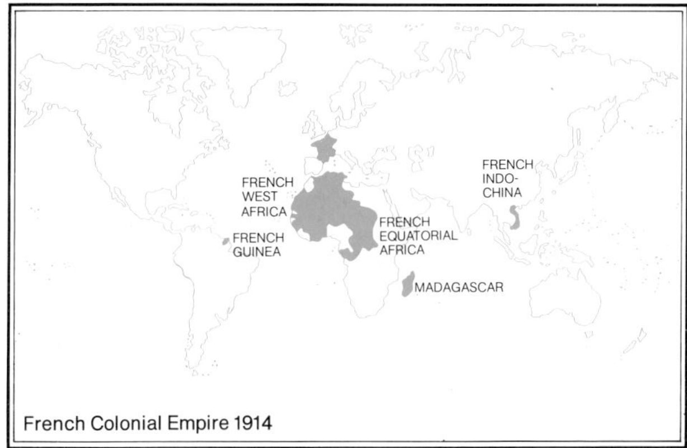

French Colonial Empire 1914

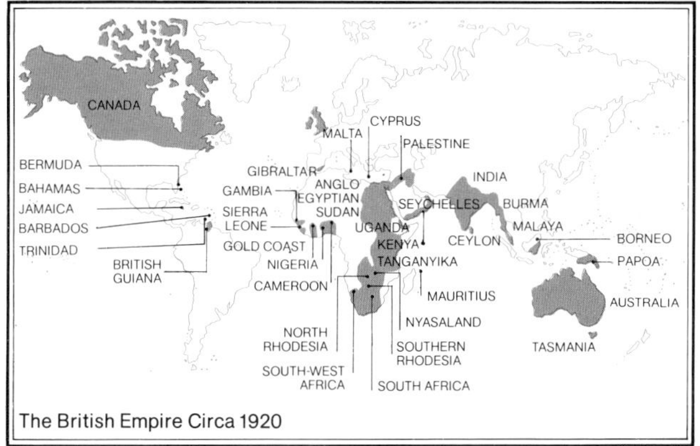

The British Empire Circa 1920

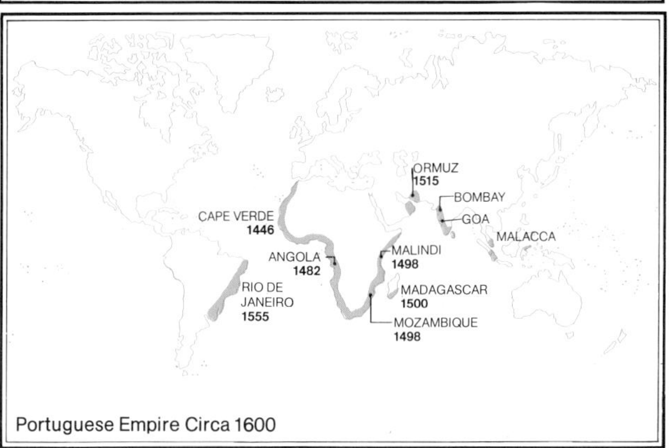

Portuguese Empire Circa 1600

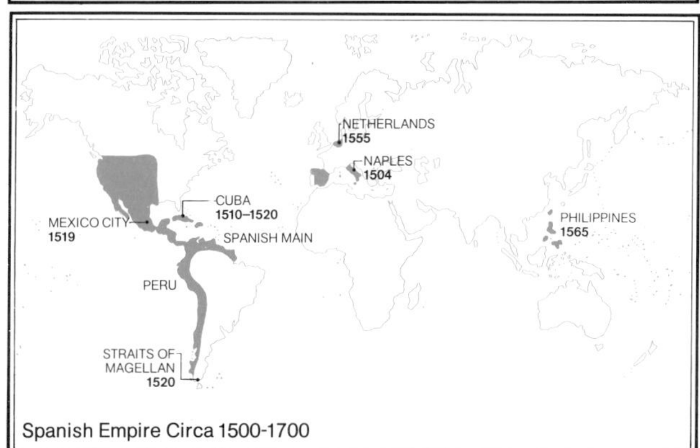

Spanish Empire Circa 1500-1700

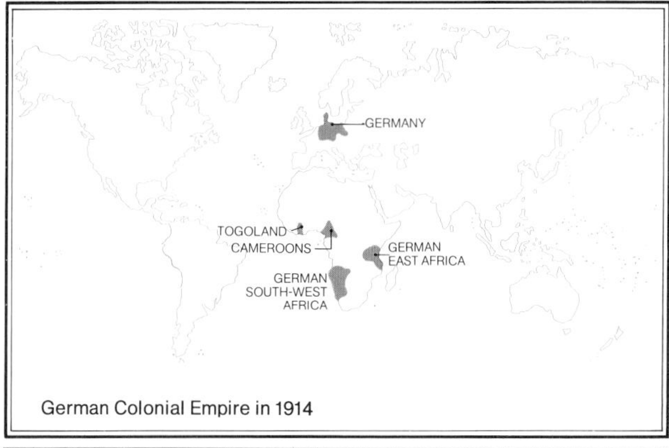

German Colonial Empire in 1914

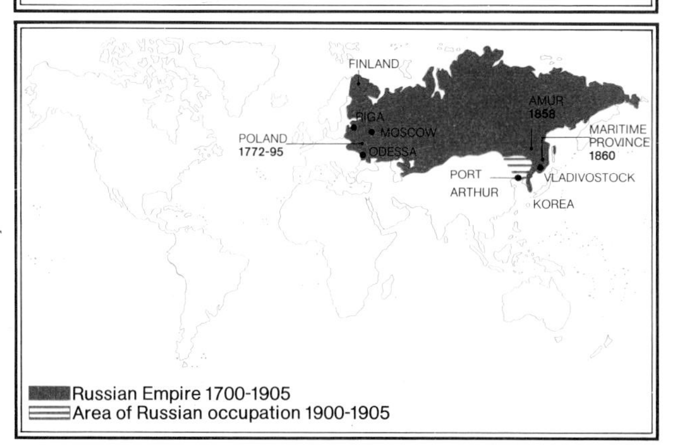

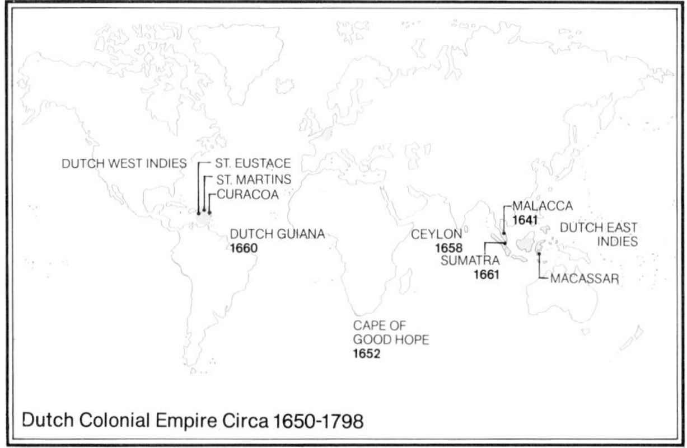

Dutch Colonial Empire Circa 1650-1798

his king, Zoser. It was adorned at the front with stone supports which foreshadowed the Greek columns of 2500 years later.

A generation after the erection of Imhotep's terraced building, the king's architects began the monumental pyramid of Gizeh. It was a tremendous leap forward from all that preceeded it. The great pyramid covers 13 acres. It is a solid mass of masonry containing 2,300,000 limestone blocks, each weighing an average of 2½ tons. The sides are 756 feet long at the base, and the building once stood 500 feet high. Herodotus wrote that a 100,000 men were working on the pyramid for twenty years. H G Wells tells us that the erection of this royal tomb left Egypt exhausted, as though by war.

The pyramids were built for the Pharaohs. No other men have been so revered. For every Pharaoh there was a tomb, and after 500 years the line of pyramids exceeded 60 miles in length.

The era of the Second Union saw advancement in every aspect of human affairs. Expeditions into Africa brought back ivory, ebony, ostrich feathers and fragrant gums and a love of beauty brought about wonderful works of art, even though perspective was still unknown. The greatest artist was the portrait sculptor and the Great Sphinx of Gizeh (which was erected at this time), still remains the largest portrait ever wrought.

The Egyptians were deeply religious. Among many gods it was Osiris, the single god of both the Nile and the sun, which they worshipped above all others. Unlike the Sumerians, whose impression of after-life was a vague, dark and foreboding world, the Egyptians believed in a very high form of after-life and it was this belief that led them onto embalming the dead and laying them in tombs.

The Second Union eventually declined. The noblemen grew to be more powerful than the Pharaohs, and Egypt entered into the second stage of its history – the feudal age. In 2450 BC the noblemen overthrew the government, and rule passed from north to south. Now pyramids appeared in the south. Man's thinking altered. A belief arose among the poor in the coming of a Messiah. For the very first time men believed that only the good could achieve happiness in the hereafter. There was drama and poetry; the earliest known books on surgery and anatomy were written; mathematics evolved; government improved; commerce spread among the Aegean islands: there was military expansion north and south, and Pharaohs of the feudal age (so called because the noblemen were like barons) proved to be rulers of great wisdom. Three of these kings bore the name Sesotris, which became one of the most illustrious names in Egyptian history. Yet once again came a decline, and a foreign people entered Egypt from Asia bringing the feudal age to an end. These were the Hykos.

Years passed and Egypt rose again, drove out the Hykos and entered its third and final age – that of empire. Thebes emerged – the powerful city. The horse came to Egypt, the chariot was mastered, and Egypt became a military empire. She conquered and controlled a vast world, and her power lasted from the 16th to the 12th century BC – a period of 400 years. But with the expansion of the Egyptian empire came the realization that the world was larger than it had previously been supposed. This led men into altering their views of the gods, and come to believe that there was only one true god.

Amenhotep III's young son, Amenhotep IV, became king about 1375 BC. He was convinced that there was only one god, and that god he believed to be the Sun-god whom he called Aton. He decreed that all should worship Aton, closed down the temples, and changed his name from Amenhotep to Ikhnaton – 'profitable to Aton'.

Eventually Ikhnaton left Thebes to build a new capital, and this he called 'Horizon of Aton'. (It is known to us as Amarna.) It was abandoned on Ikhnaton's death, and his son-in-law – for Ikhnaton had no son of his own – became king. His name was Tutenkhaton – 'living image of Aton' – and he was possibly only twelve years old when Ikhnaton died. He was taken back to Thebes by the revengeful priests of the old god, Amon, and made to change his name from Tutenkhaton to Tutenkh*amon*. He died when he was 18. It is possible that he was murdered. He was the last of the most powerful Pharaohs that Egypt had ever seen. His tomb, through the miracle of being accidentally covered over, was the only tomb not to be plundered, and it was discovered intact and completely undisturbed in 1922.

Following Tutenkhamon were Seti I and Ramses II, but Egypt was in a state of decline, and they were unable to drive the invading Hittites out of Syria, for the raiders from Asia possessed iron, while Egypt was the last great power of the Age of Bronze. Egypt fell. She had risen to great heights; she had mercenaries fighting for her; she herself had lost interest in war, but she could not escape it. When Mediterranean invaders gathered against her, and in the middle of the 12th century BC, Egypt collapsed.

Following the fall of Babylon to the Kassites, and the parallel with the development of Egypt, the people of the northern city kingdom of Assur slowly arose – the Assyrians, a dark haired, thick lipped and long nosed people. They had been taught by the Sumerians, and had fought for control of their city for almost 1,000 years. The strain of war toughened them. Early on the Assyrian kings introduced the chariot to their army, and they emerged as the strongest military force the world had yet seen. Simultaneously, trade with all the neighboring nations made them wealthy. Silver was mined in Cilicia and greatly improved commerce.

In that 1,000 years, the Assyrians had fought with the Mitannians, a ferocious military state which had held Nineveh for a time, and the Hattites, the wealthy Phoenician city-kingdoms of the Mediterranean east coast. In the 16th century BC, they had to face the dangerous hostility of a new nomadic people, the

Hebrews. North of them were the Arameans, or Syrians, who occupied Syria. The Hebrews, who had suffered greatly at the hands of the Egyptians, eventually gained all of the country of Palestine. Kingdoms flourished beneath both peoples, the most powerful among the Arameans being that of Damascus.

There followed a peaceful penetration of Aramean commerce far into western Asia, and with them they took and spread an alphabetic writing which they had probably borrowed from the Phoenicians, or the Canaanites. They possessed the Egyptian pen and ink, and it passed down the Euphrates to Persia and even penetrated to the frontiers of India, supplying the east Indians with their Sanskrit alphabet.

The Assyrians and Arameans worked together in business and government, and Aramaic finally became the language of the whole group of nations. It was the language later spoken by Jesus.

Assyria waited patiently to inherit the empire of the east. She watched with delight the collapse of her two greatest rivals – Egypt and the Hittites – the Hittites who had influenced the early Agean world, and had passed coinage and the beginnings of architecture onto the Greeks. When they and the Egyptians fell, the Assyrians rose, at first unable to conquer the powerful group of Aramean, Phoenician and Hebrew kingdoms, but rising above them in 722 BC under a king who raised the Assyrian empire to heights of grandeur – Sargon the Second. He was succeeded by Sennacherib, Esarhaddon and Assurbanipal (called Sardanapalus by the Greeks) and they made the Assyrian empire the most magnificent so far known. Great conquests were made. Nineveh became the capital, and formed the first stage of advanced architecture in Asia. It had libraries, but its art was a brutal art, void of any tenderness – a reflection of the terrible harshness of the Assyrian society. Punishments for law-breakers, apart from death, listed also the amputation of fingers, ears and noses, as well as the tearing out of eyes and tongues. The international situation the Assyrian dominion created gave the Hebrews their deeply influential concepts of a god – ideas destined to affect the whole of man's later history.

Slowly, economic and agricultural decline crippled the Assyrian empire, and then it fell beneath the peoples who challenged it. The Chaldeans rose, and they were to be the last of the Semitic empires.

In 604 BC their great emperor, Nebuchadnezzar began a reign which lasted over forty years, and he restored Babylon and made it the colorful and magnificent city we imagine it to have been.

Civilization progressed considerably under the Chaldeans. The days of the week were named after the celestial bodies, and we still use those names today. Only one or two have changed. The Chaldeans worshipped the heavenly bodies, and while *Satur*day was sacred to Saturn, the Sun was sacred to *Sun*day, the moon to *Mon*day, and so on. Other times brought us Norse names for a few of our days (i.e. Thursday – *Thors'*day).

The astronomer, Nau-rimannu, among many remarkable achievements, calculated the exact length of the year to be 365 days, 6 hours and 41 seconds – two thousand years before the invention of the telescope. His measurement was only 26 minutes and 55 seconds too long.

He compiled tables of the revolutions of the sun and moon, and a century later, the astronomer Kidinnu followed up his work with greater accuracy, making advances in other directions himself, and proving the variance of the length of the year as measured from equinox to equinox, and as measured between two successive arrivals of the earth at its nearest point to the sun.

And while the Chaldeans made these advances, the Phoenicians continued to whisper around and about the ancient world like flies, spreading the disease of culture wherever they traded, and infesting the minds of scattered men with the ailments of his more learned, distant brother.

Ideas were growing and uniting and dividing men. The Hebrews spoke of a brotherhood of all men; values changed, and small pieces of the giant jig-saw of nature began to slip together and as men learnt, so they realized the minuteness of themselves.

The Chaldeans dimmed and faded. The Persians appeared, and after them the Greeks and the Romans. After the Greeks but before the end of the Roman Empire, a man by the name of Jesus Christ appeared and walked around his small corner of the earth for 33 years. He was never forgotten. All three influenced the later history of western man – they all gave of themselves, and small parts of them were accepted and absorbed, and this is really the heritage of western culture.

Civilizations appear and rule, and disappear. Their ways of living are rarely adopted by other societies, but often pieces of their cultures are. Ideas are inherited, borrowed and shaped and chiseled. Sciences are pursued, and the knowledge which springs from their study passed on.

We do not live as the Greeks lived, but we read their philosophers, their dramatists, and we are influenced by them. We do not have the Roman arena, and do not delight in watching lions savage humans, yet our administration resembles that of the Romans in certain, basic areas. We enjoy the arts they possessed and have left us – their ideas are not unknown to us. We live as we believe right, and they lived as they believed right, and just as the Romans and the Greeks were blind to a destiny, so are we. When man changed from being a food gatherer to a food producer, he laid the first stone of the pyramid of culture. Throughout history it has grown. Some of the stones are ugly, others cracked and chipped, others smooth and clean.

Population and the future

Some of our population – growing at an increasing rate and reckoned to be 7,000 million by the year 2000 AD – crowd at a stadium at Colombes, France.

The game of prophecy is, notoriously, a mug's game. The human future is a mystery: perhaps the only thing that we can say about it with any certainty is that it will be full of surprises, as the human story has always been in the past.

Nevertheless, it seems overwhelmingly probable that as the 20th century draws towards its close, the character of our story will be more and more determined by the factor of population. Our numbers are larger than they have ever been before, and they are increasing at an explosive rate: various attempts have already been made, and will be made more vigorously in the future, to lower birth rates and thus bring the 'population explosion' under control. But it is far from clear that these attempts will have anything more than a local or marginal kind of success. If we try to imagine what our world and our life-style will be in the year 2000 the first fact that we have to take into account is that the world will be a great deal more crowded than it is now, and that life-styles everywhere will be modified and largely governed by this situation.

This raises serious problems that are, curiously, self-inflicted. They stem from what can fairly be called 'man's conquest of nature' from the scientific, technological and economic achievements of the modern world. Nature has her own way of controlling populations, of preventing them from expanding beyond what the environment can carry. Nature's methods, though cruel, are effective. We have always had a high birth rate, but it was offset by high death rates, especially in infancy. While our numbers have been increasing, slowly and erratically, since the very beginning and while particular cities and regions might be crowded and hungry there was never, until recently, any population problem. Overall there was ample space and potential food for everybody. The world is a big place, after all.

But over the last two or three hundred years, and especially in the 20th century – we have started to interfere seriously with nature's methods of population control. We still have high birth rates. But thanks to medicine, sanitation, public health, industrialization, and a much improved standard of living, we now have a much lower death rate throughout most of the world.

Our numbers are therefore increasing sharply, and on the mathematical principle of compound interest: they are increasing at a rate which is itself increasing sharply. The point is not that we have more babies but that far more of them survive to have babies of their own. Suddenly we have come up against the fact that the world is less large than we had supposed. There are limits beyond which the world cannot possibly be made to provide more water and food and living-space. Those limits are now in sight. The growth of our species is like that of a man whose natural growth has accelerated so sharply that he was bumping his head on the ceiling before he knew what was happening. There cannot be

Population and the future

The world population growth curve estimates nearly 6,000 million people by 2000 AD. The map below shows those countries expanding quickest.

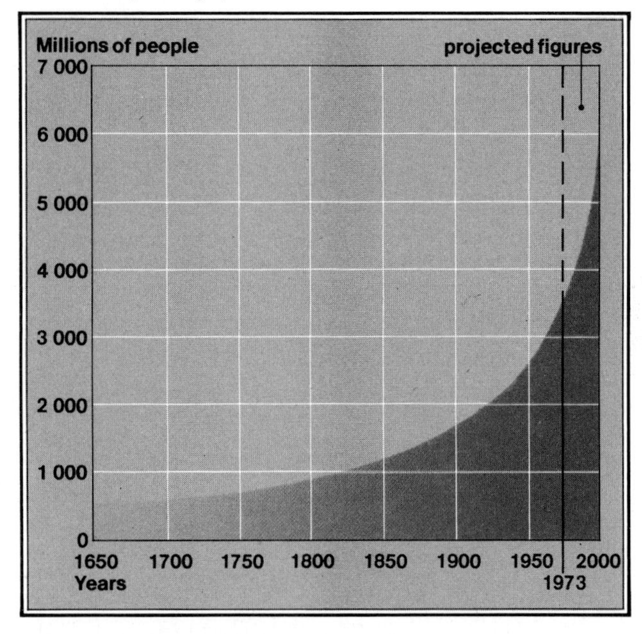

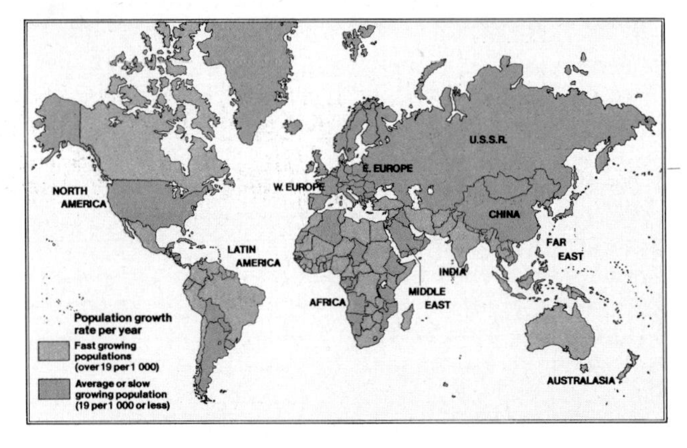

unlimited growth in a closed system. We are confronted by a short-fused 'population bomb' which is likely to explode in our children's life-time if not in our own. We run into serious difficulties, however, if we try to work out what is actually going to happen. There are too many unknown quantities for us to form a picture of our world and life-style in the year 2000. We cannot really prophesy. We can only make a series of plausible guesses, each one based upon its own hypothetical foundation.

It took an immeasurably long time – from neolithic times until about 1600 AD – for the world's population to reach its first billion (1,000 million). The second billion was reached after only another 300 years, around 1900, and the third after a mere 50 years. At the time of writing, it seems that the fourth billion will be reached only 30 years later, in 1980, and that the total population of the planet will be some 7,000 million by the end of the century.

These figures, however, based upon extrapolation from present trends, need cautious handling. The principle of compound interest does not operate in a vacuum and, taken by itself, leads to absurd conclusions. Dr Paul Ehrlich describes an imaginary situation – not in this century, but not too long after it – in which we shall all be jostling one another, shoulder to shoulder, all over the world. Looking still further ahead, he imagines a time when everything in the visible universe would be converted into people, and the ball of people would be expanding with the speed of light. The pure mathematics of compound interest and the exponential curve do indeed point to such conclusions. But, obviously, it is not going to happen like that. It is nowhere seriously disputed that new factors will come into the picture at some point, and that the world's population will level off, and perhaps drop sharply, in the fairly near future.

The 7,000 million figure for the year 2000 can be regarded as plausible only on the basis of three questionable assumptions. The first of these is that no major nuclear war takes place. As we all know the major powers have stockpiled nuclear weapons on a scale that threatens our whole race. It is all too easy, in this unstable world, to imagine a very brief war after which the survivors – if any – would have no 'population problem' beyond that of struggling to remain in existence. The second assumption is that major epidemics and plagues are things of the past. We could be wrong here. The influenza virus presents one danger out of many. From time to time new mutants of this virus come into existence and the speed and universality of air transport ensures that they spread rapidly all over the world, causing epidemics which have been limited in their impact – so far. It is worth remembering that the influenza epidemic after World War I, helped along by the exhaustion and malnutrition following the war, killed more people than were killed in the war itself. It is possible that a comparable epidemic, caused by some new mutation of the old virus, might sweep through the

The waste land will soon bear yet more Americans but the explosion, in the event of nuclear war or uncontrolled epidemics, may never come.

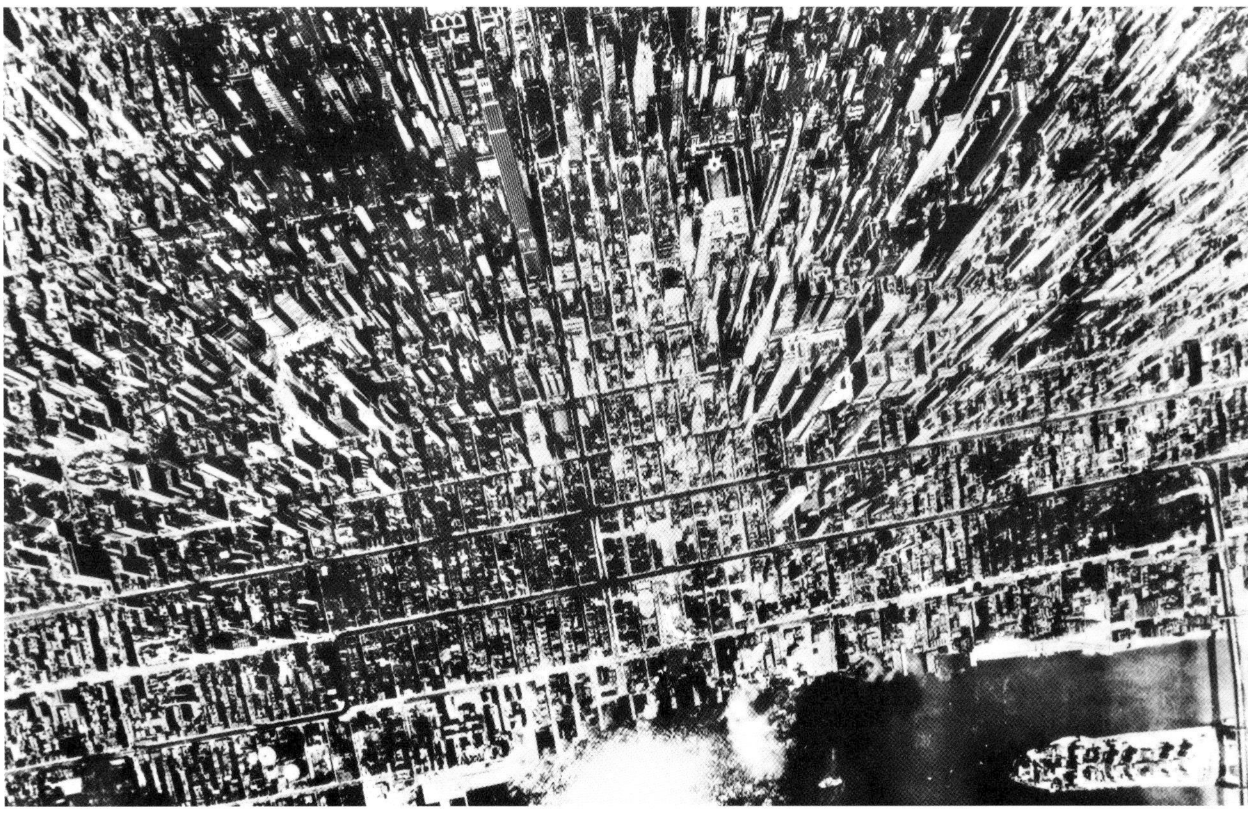

An aerial view of New York – now the third largest city after Shanghai and Tokyo – reveals its greatest difference from London: its dearth of parks.

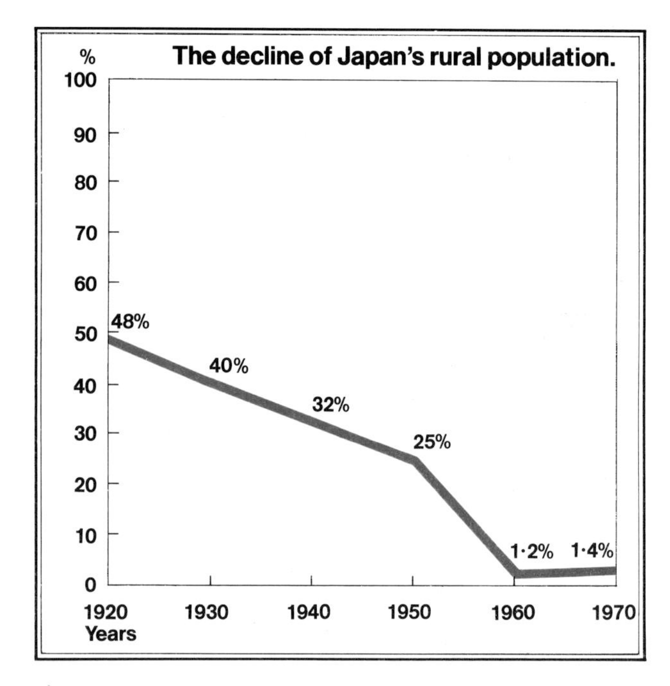

world at any time in future, propagating itself so rapidly that it would outpace and overwhelm all attempts at immunization and cure. The survivors might face a real problem of under-population.

The third assumption is that the medical, social and economic factors which have achieved our present low death rate will remain operative. These largely depend upon the complex fragile web of civilization, which might be endangered by an environmental crisis – particularly by an energy-crisis – by social unrest and disruption, by some ideological shift in values and priorities, or by any or all of these factors in combination. Increasing hunger, as the world becomes more crowded, is a major danger that can lead to widespread and chronic malnutrition, rendering people more vulnerable to epidemics and plagues. Starvation would also mean that securing food – by more intensive agriculture, and probably by aggressive war against richer neighbors – would be given priority in relation to the factors which ensure low death rates.

If, as indeed may happen, we find ourselves living in the year 2000 along with 7,000 million other people what will our lives be like?

The more crowded world of the year 2000 is certainly likely to be stressful, particularly when and where men insist on crowding into increasingly unmanageable cities and making technological development into a way of life. Where, however, life becomes simpler, more decentralized and regional, more 'primitive', the stresses of a crowded world may become considerably more endurable.

The human race may learn this lesson in good time and put it into effect before the event. But it would involve a universal and profound change of heart and habit not only in the developed countries but perhaps also in those 'developing' countries which are already on the dead-end path followed by Europe and North America.

Clearly, if the harmful effects of overpopulation are to be avoided birth rates have got to be lowered – everywhere and permanently. Advocates of population control, though strong on urgency, tend to be weak on plausibility. Gandhi, and in a sense Malthus, proposed that population should be controlled by a moral revolution – by universal sexual restraint. It seems unlikely that this will ever happen and unfortunately the same seems true of many of the proposals for birth control that are canvassed today. No amount of contraceptive equipment and information will stabilize any population without compulsion, or else a general tendency for people to desire small families. Within totalitarian societies, some kind of compulsion may be possible: in China, for example, birth rates have already been sharply reduced. But in much of the world there is a deep-seated urge to have more than three or four children. Over the uncountable millennia during which the survival of the tribe could be ensured in no other way, the tendency to want a large family has been instilled in human nature. It is unlikely that even the heaviest campaign of propaganda and inducement could reverse this tendency except locally, marginally and temporarily. And this will not be enough. And if population control does not operate permanently and universally not only will the plan to de-fuse the 'population bomb' be ineffective, but the groups which do control their population will in the long run simply be out-bred and overwhelmed by the groups which do not. Population control, unless permanent and universal, may be self-defeating.

Many people place great hope in what is called the demographic transition. They point to the well-established tendency for birth rates to decline as living standards rise. They argue that the population problem can best be tackled indirectly by improving living standards throughout the world, especially in the poorer countries. The richer part of the world, however, at present displays no intention of devoting anything more than a minute proportion of its efforts to this end. Even if the richer nations underwent a change of heart, it is unlikely that they could ever bring the whole world to anything like the present European or American standard of living, and thus to their lowered birth rates.

The probabilities seem to point in the other direction. The economic gap between the richer countries with their low birth rates and the poorer countries with their high birth rates is already wide and is becoming wider. But it is as likely to be closed – eventually – by the rich becoming poorer as by the poor becoming richer. If rich countries become poorer the 'demographic transition' will be reversed and the birth rates of these countries can be expected to rise again accordingly.

As cities become more crowded so the problem of stress increases, as in Tokyo. But much of the world's surface is sparsely populated.

As production increases more and more goods are transported round the world, but the gap between rich and poor countries continues to increase.

People living in crowded cities need the peace and quiet of the surrounding countryside and most, like these Tokyo citizens, succeed.

Man in 2000 AD

Sun City, built in the clean, dry desert air of Arizona provides homes mainly for the retired. By 2000 AD cities will be bigger.

Most speculation about the distant future – typically represented by the symbolic year 2000 – is characterized by a strong emphasis on change, particularly change impelled by new technology. But in fact a concentration on continuity may be more useful in forecasting the future daily life of western man. There will be many new and changed technologies, but almost all of these will be new means of achieving old ends and will have very little effect on daily life. The year 2000 is no longer a long way off. Most people alive today will live to see it, and few will find it alien. Look back the same distance of time to the mid-20th century – has daily life in western cities changed very much? Even looking back a full half century to the 1920s we see very little change in the daily life of the middle classes. To be sure, the working classes have changed their life very much in this century; they have largely achieved middle class standards and style of life. The changes of the past half century have been very gradual and incremental. There is little reason to expect more rapid or significant change in the next 25 years or even the next half century. The most important trends are well established and probably irreversible in anything resembling a free society.

A surprise-free projection must center on continued urbanization. To speak of western man will be to speak of all western men. The peasant as he has been known will scarcely exist. The farmer will be a highly skilled technician, using advanced materials and equipment. Any special status he may retain will merely reflect romantic nostalgia. Cities will continue to grow and spread and rural areas to decay. This process, very nearly completed in north-west Europe, North America and the antipodes, will continue in southern and eastern Europe and in the westernistic areas of Asia, Latin America and Africa.

Cities will grow both in population and in area. London, New York and Tokyo will have over twenty million people. In the ten to twenty range will be Paris, Chicago, Los Angeles, and the ring city of the Netherlands. The most rapid population growth, however, will be achieved in cities of between one and ten million people, for example, Melbourne, Houston, Madrid, Marseilles. The most striking population gains will be in regions of mild and even semi-tropical climate which offer superior recreational opportunities and a better physical environment than the cold iron-and-coal cities of the early industrial era. The last quarter of the 20th century should also see the rapid development of smaller urban centers of 100,000 to one million people within driving time of the larger cities. Freeways and high-speed trains will make it possible for people to combine the advantages of small city living with access to the superior cosmopolitan high culture and mass culture facilities of larger centers.

Cities will continue to spread in area more rapidly than they grow in population. The extension of modern high-

As suburban transport improves, city density – as reflected in the World Trade Building, Wall Street, New York – will be less.

Alcoholics have always been part of the city scene and there is no sign of drinking abating. By 2000 AD beer and wine will be more popular.

ways and increased availability of automobiles will permit a larger and larger part of the population to achieve the ancient ambition of being a landowner. The era of the automobile is by no means over, indeed it has just begun. Doubtless the individual motor vehicle of the year 2000 will not be powered by the type of internal combustion engine we know today. Emission-free and generally more efficient power sources are just beginning to be seriously developed. The engines of the year 2000 will have a generation of concentrated research effort and capital investment behind them. Motorways and freeways will permit the almost endless spread of cities. Overall metropolitan densities will drop toward 3,000 per square mile or perhaps even lower. The very line between city and country will disappear, particularly as more and more people obtain a second home in mountain, lake, seashore and desert areas.

While academics in the year 2000 will continue to draw maps of 'conurbation' and 'megalopolis' this 'urban sprawl' will be largely open area occupied by a few scattered houses on country lanes not too far from major traffic arteries, shopping centers, factories and office blocks, schools and parks. The great mass of the population will opt for this life although many will be nostalgic both for the countryside and for the medieval and early industrial high-density city. Substantial minorities, particularly the young and/or restless will choose high-density cosmopolitan living in the centers of old cities. Others, sick of the anonymity and conflict of urban life, will withdraw into the countryside; but most of the alienated will attempt to retreat into individual family units and inward-looking sub-communities within the megalopolis.

The urban landscape will look no more different from today than ours does from 1950. The subway systems will still be there, probably running on rubber wheels with air-conditioned cars. The roads and plazas will remain, although a few will be closed to vehicular traffic. Almost all the parks, museums and churches will survive. There will be some new buildings and other facilities in older areas but most of what is new will have been built on the fringes. Fire and redevelopment will have taken their toll but most of today's buildings will still stand. In 2000 the leading architects will have long since abandoned today's ubiquitous sterile style – in favour of what, we cannot say; perhaps in favor of functional computer-designed building systems, or, less likely, classical or romantic revivals.

Homes will be little different from today. The free-standing, owner-occupied, single family house will remain the ideal, and that ideal will have been achieved by a majority of the populace. Nary a house will lack complete plumbing, central heating, and full utilities. The typical house will have more floor space than today's and each member of the family will expect his own room. Specialized rooms for individual and collective activities

The expansion of Detroit from 1900 to 2000 AD reflects the growth of cities everywhere, but increased prosperity will lead to more country homes.

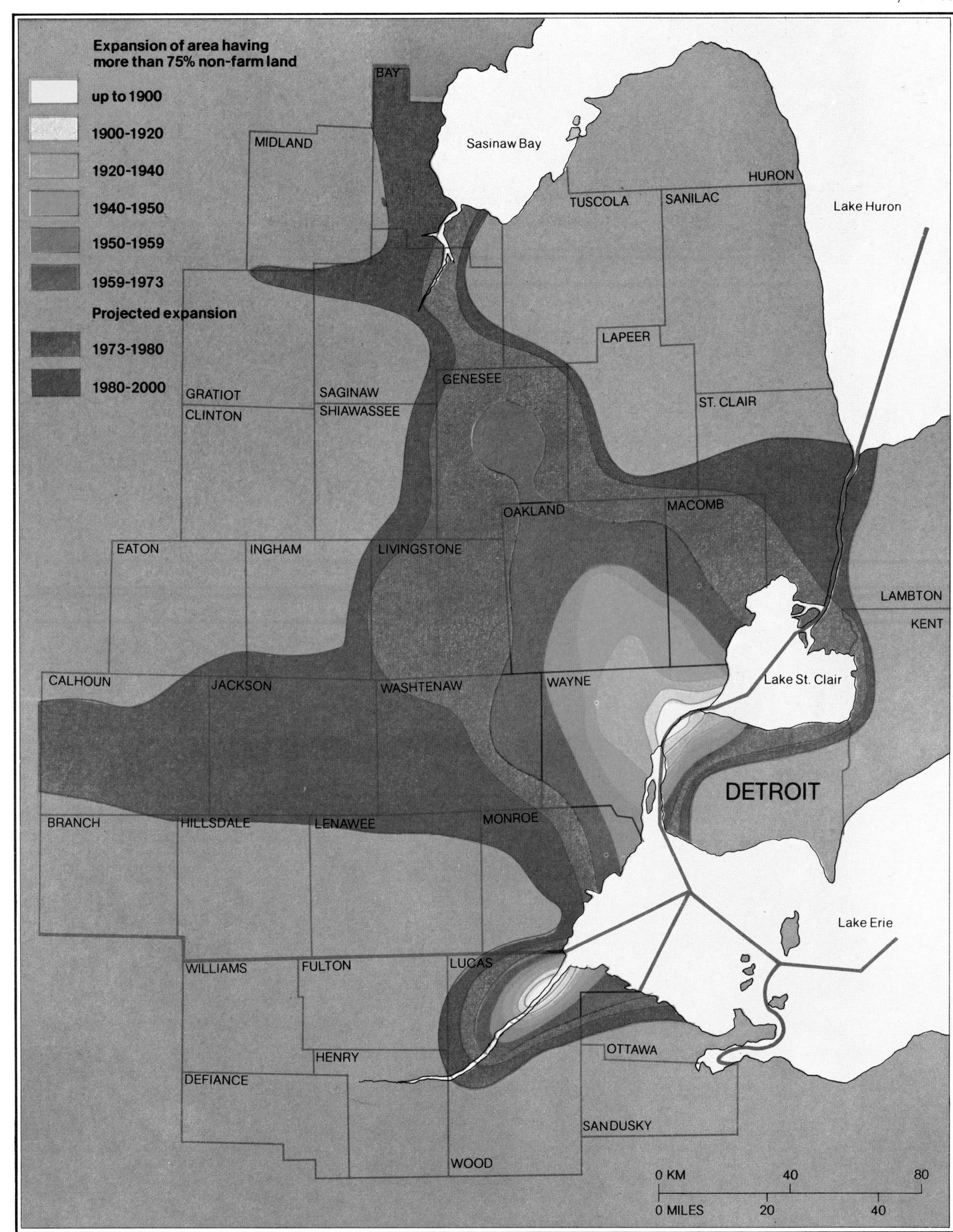

A model of a plexiglass hexahedron city, which would stand 3,500 feet high and house 170,000 people on less than half a square mile.

will also be more prevalent. Houses will be easier to clean and maintain on a daily basis because of near universal air conditioning, dust-free design, and superior chemical and electrical cleaning techniques, but will be much more complex and subject to major breakdown. They will be thick with wiring for life-support, maintenance, communication, and entertainment systems. The householder or homemaker will have to be a skilled technician to keep them running. Formal courses will probably be offered in 'home engineering' in secondary schools in Britain and the continent, and in universities in America and Scandinavia.

Communications will be greatly improved by the year 2000. Picture telephones will be the principal means of personal communication. The rich will have their homes wired for more exotic systems. The advent of multi-channel cable television and TV cassettes, together with much larger TV screens and/or projectors, will probably kill the movie house, but will permit a commercial flourishing of the arts as highly specialized forms of entertainment – baroque or country music for example – which will be available nationally or internationally through specialized channels and/or recording devices. I say a 'commercial' flourishing because no one today can write a credible scenario for a revival of high culture; new varieties of nihilism and Alexandrian pastiches are all that can be expected.

People will continue to live, work, learn and play in separate locations. The home will remain the single most important place and the nuclear family will continue to be the most important focus of life. Men will see themselves as husbands, fathers and breadwinners; women as wives and mothers. It will be taken for granted that women work, but it would not be wise at this time to assume much further breakdown in the traditional family structure. Probably by the year 2000 we will have gone through several cycles of 'liberated' and family-centered ideologies for women. Nevertheless, by historical standards, the birth rate will be relatively low, families will be relatively small, and less of people's lives will be spent as parents. Divorce will be commonplace, and probably trial marriage and other informal sexual relationships also. Deviant sexual behavior will be more openly displayed and tolerated, but only indulged in by small minorities. These will be modest, slow changes to which few should have difficulty in adjusting. Although there will probably be a 'puritan' reaction before the end of the century, traditional standards will not be restored.

Work will also be a central aspect of self-identity. We can reasonably project that urban man in the year 2000 will, however, work a shorter part of the week and fewer years of his life as people live longer, the age of retirement is lowered, and the period of education is prolonged. There will be slow shifts in job classifications over the next generation. There will be fewer manual jobs and more manipulating of words, numbers and people. There is a good chance that, as in some parts of California today, people will be identified more by their play than by their work. That a person is a skier, a chess player or a theater buff will be more important than whether he is a lawyer, a mechanic, or a scholar. As today, most people will work to earn money to satisfy other needs, but will not normally object excessively to their jobs.

Most of the west will have what is now the standard of living of the upper middle classes but not their satisfaction of being better off than the herd. The very rich and/or powerful, of course, will have more luxuries and privileges than the rest. There will still be poor people in cities who will appear disadvantaged compared to the majority, but most of the western working classes will have followed their North American and Scandinavian counterparts in achieving middle class living standards. The 'poor' of the year 2000 will only be relatively poor, having achieved all that is necessary for healthy subsistence. Their 'problems' will consist of the real and perceived psychic damage of having fewer luxuries than the rest of society. We may expect some leveling of incomes through government taxation, transfer payments, and services provided directly to everyone on a subsidized or 'free' basis.

In one way the cities will be far better than they are today. They will be almost entirely free of air and water pollution and, to a lesser extent, noise pollution. Control of air and water pollutants has already been shown to be cheap and effective even though the technological effort has just begun. By the year 2000 emission controls will be taken for granted. Recycling and other economic usage of solid wastes will also be commonplace. In areas which lack ground water the recycling of water waste and/or desalination of sea-water will provide more than enough water for everyone. The technology is already well established.

Because of improvements in air and water quality, as well as steady incremental advances in medicine, people will be healthier, even without major breakthroughs in heart disease and cancer. But although objectively healthier than today, the populace is likely to be subjectively worse off as new forms of previously unrecognized ailments are identified and made the subject of public concern by public health officials, researchers and publicists. Mental health will probably be an even worse problem as most people achieve an educational and income level high enough to be troubled by such luxuries as 'neuroses'. Although a cycle or two of 'return to religion' and 'rediscovery of values' will have been undergone by AD 2000, it is almost certain that the west will be more secular than today. Soon the penetration of secular humanism into the masses of Europe, North America, and the antipodes will have pretty thoroughly substituted 'sickness' for 'evil' as the explanation for the world's and the individual's shortcomings. As in the past most people will theoretically accept and operationally disregard the prevailing ideology. Secular humanism is very thin sustenance for the spirit; millions will find solace in richer religious gruel. All manner of old and new sects and religious substitutes should flourish. Still, most people will continue to be devoted to thoughtless materialism and harmless superstition.

One aspect of daily life in 2000 certain to trouble many people today will be the commonplace reliance on chemical and perhaps even electrical means of modifying individual behavior. Psychotics and criminals will be routinely 'treated'. Individual citizens will take all manner of mind- and body-affecting drugs as commonly as they smoke today. (By 2000 the anti-nicotine crusade will probably have long since peaked and ebbed.) Alcohol will still be the most favored solace. An anti-hangover remedy ought to be available – one of the few unmitigated boons of the 20th century.

While we may reasonably be sceptical about some of the more exotic possibilities of biochemistry such as cloning, some very modest accomplishments will have noticeable effects on everyday life. Cosmetics and plastic surgery will permit the ugly or bored to make major alterations in their personal appearances. More complex transplanted and/or artificial organs will be available. Nearly 100 per cent effective and safe birth control will be easily obtained, although young people will still slip in moments of adolescent passion. Prior sex determination of children will also be practical, if only through very early fetal sex identification plus abortion, leading to a short-term overproduction of boys and consequent tight regulation – which might be the opening wedge for child delivery licensing.

Overpopulation will not be a real problem in the rich west. Despite the warnings of prophets of doom of the early 1970s there will be more than sufficient raw materials, water and fuel for everyone. New technologies will achieve many substitutions and make available materials which are now uneconomical to extract. The citizen may have to pay more, but he will be able to afford to. A more serious problem in the year 2000 will be tourist pollution. Huge jet aircraft will be dumping millions of people into desirable tourist areas. In addition to being accustomed to the presence of foreign visitors, urban man at the end of the century will take for granted the use of foreign goods, and through the media he will be made aware of events in other cities. To this degree, the world will be, not a global village in which everyone knows everyone, but a 'global city' where one is in continual contact with strangers.

More regulation of the individual can be anticipated. Although this factor will be exaggerated by those who feel they have an interest in regulation, society will be somewhat more complex. Also, society in the year 2000 will have a slightly older, adult population, certainly more concerned with security and less willing to take risks than a younger society. 'Consumer protection', 'health', and 'safety' laws will hedge about every sort of activity. It will be increasingly difficult to introduce new technologies because the officials responsible for pre-screening products will be able to find ways in which they could be harmful. 'Preventive medicine' may surround everyday life with a myriad of restrictions. Many individuals of course will continue to be smarter and more devious than the bureaucrats, and lawbreaking will be widespread. Indeed, the complexity of regulations will probably make it practically impossible to carry on everyday life without continuously violating laws. We can expect some leveling within the western world – as Americans become more accustomed to having European levels of social control and American-style 'lawlessness' spreads to north-eastern Europe.

However, a much more serious and more widely accepted form of social control will be that occasioned by the fear of individual acts of nihilism and terrorism, which should continue to increase as individuals feel more 'liberated' and the habits of obedience engendered by the Baroque state and its bourgeois successors are forgotten. Outright terrorism is not the worst threat. Our complex systems require a higher level of co-ordination and reliability. A few saboteurs, even acting non-violently, can disrupt the lives of millions. One form of disruptive behavior – strikes by workers in vital monopoly industries such as transportation or utilities – is likely not to be permitted, at least not legally, by the year 2000.

What about alternatives? Note the caveat at the end of my first paragraph: 'in anything resembling a free society.' This projection describes an increased standard of living for the bulk of the population. It also, however, means a decay in the standard of living for the privileged classes. More wealth and mobility for the masses means they have access to goods, services, places, and functions previously reserved for the élite. The natural dissatisfaction of the prosperous will be reflected in virulent criticisms of the entire system. To the extent that states are undemocratic – particularly when controlled by the 'bureaucratic bourgeoisie' – attempts will be made to halt the process described above. These may succeed, particularly if there should be massive social dislocations in the early 1980s. Anarchy, terrorism and perhaps even revolution and war would lend much support to whoever could promise social stability and leave little tolerance to persons continuing to advocate 'freedom' which would be interpreted as support for further turmoil and upheaval.

And we ought not to forget another scenario: although every year the probability is very low, there could be a thermo-nuclear war. Megatonnage is the ultimate retort to megalopolis. If the politicians fumble there will be no urban daily life in the year 2000. The development of two hundred years would be liquidated. Once again the western world would be dominated by the husbandman and the artisan, and perhaps even the priest and the warrior.

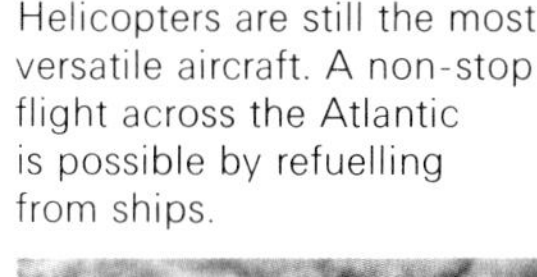

Helicopters are still the most versatile aircraft. A non-stop flight across the Atlantic is possible by refuelling from ships.

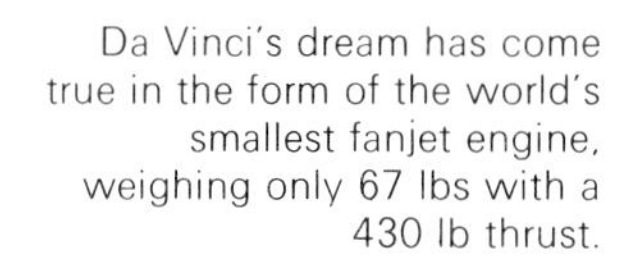

Da Vinci's dream has come true in the form of the world's smallest fanjet engine, weighing only 67 lbs with a 430 lb thrust.

Cockerell's hovercraft invention has enormous potential on land and sea and as an everyday means of getting around.

Tomorrow's society

To counter the 'dehumanising' factors in modern life, groups at the Esalen Institute in California take exercises in heightening awareness.

The forecaster must be wary of projecting his personal idiosyncracies and values upon the future. He must, in speculating about the prospects for culture, recognize that many of his readers will believe that he is predicting what he wishes to happen. Let it be emphasized, therefore, that most of the trends which will be forecast for the west do not reflect wishful thinking on the part of the writer. Some trends he likes, others are odious to him. But even within this limited space, a case can be made that, like it or not, this is the way the world is going. Let us begin with discussion of certain elements of Hudson Institute's long-term multifold trend (H Kahn & B Bruce-Briggs, *Things to Come*, New York 1972). We shall be limited here to cultural aspects of this trend, those aspects which have to do with widely-held values and forms of artistic expression, but not aspects directly derived from technology or social organization. Several central long-term trends have been proceeding with some ebbs and flows for the past millennium and most observers of western history would agree with most of these, although certainly they would disagree with some of the terminology. Particularly controversial might be the use of Pitirim Sorokin's concept of sensate culture (*Social and Cultural Dynamics* New York 1937). This term might be best understood by contrasting it to his other concept, ideational. To Sorokin ideational cultures are principally motivated by other worldly ideals. They tend to be charismatic, commonistic, emotional, and spiritual. They rely upon revelation of dogma for truth. In western history, the early Middle Ages represents an extremely ideational culture. On the other hand, a sensate culture is empirical, secular, humanistic, pragmatic, utilitarian, contractual and oriented to this world rather than to the next. Over the past 1,000 years western culture has experienced a steady, though irregular, movement from the ideational to the sensate. Few modern artists and writers approach religious themes and contemporary religion tends to be pragmatic and worldly, looking to man rather than to God.

A trend toward an increasingly sensate culture means a growing role for science and technology and a systematic erosion of the sacred. It can be argued persuasively that ever since the 11th century the role of sacred perspectives and attitudes has been waning and the role of the secular, practical and humanist perspectives and attitudes has been growing.

The clearest reflection of a sensate trend is the nearly unchecked spread of secular humanism – the religion of humanity as prefigured by the *philosophes* and codified by the positivists. Key dogmas of secular humanism are the glorification of man and reason, the denial of God and original sin, and the establishment of worldly life, liberty and the pursuit of happiness as the proper aims of the individual and society. It is the religion of the Marxist nations and the United States. A generation ago it overcame Facism; in the last few years it has appeared

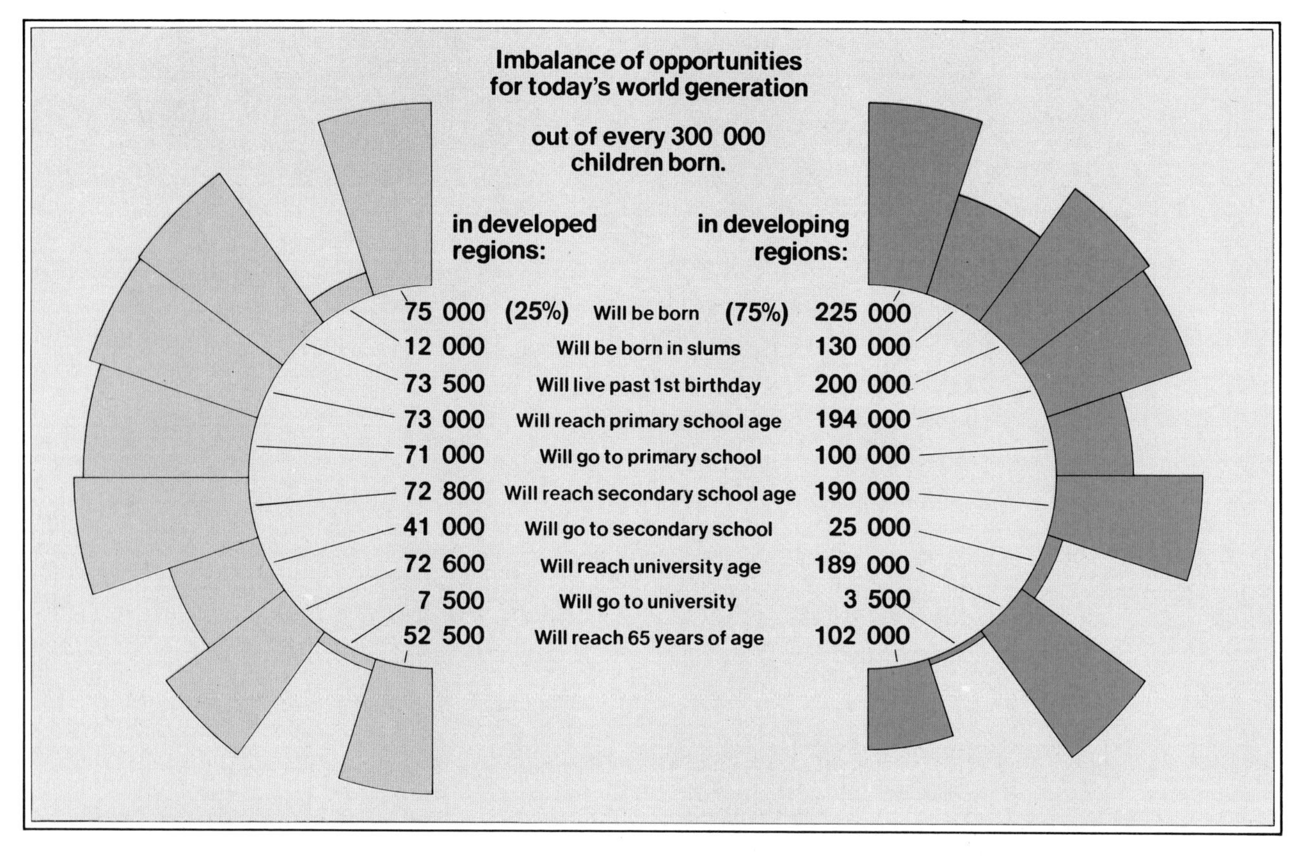

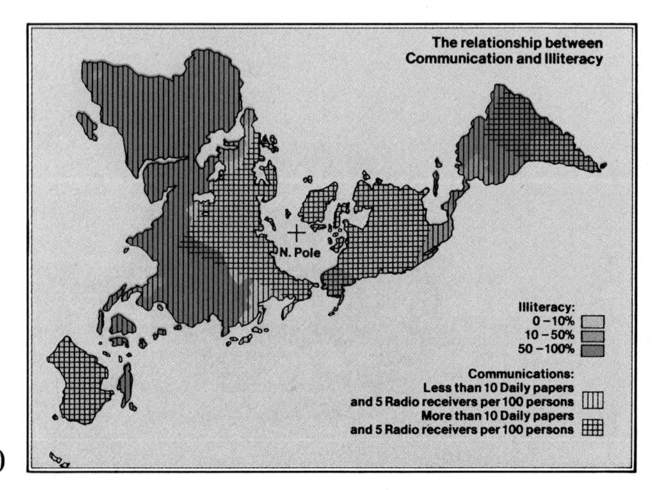

in the Roman Church; it is penetrating all of the previously religious traditional societies; and it presently has no serious rivals, save nationalism. Secular humanism is nevertheless thin sustenance for the soul, and many persons will seek stronger faiths – witness the current vigorous prospering of exotic oriental cults and fundamentalist Protestant sects among the most advanced elements of the west.

Today we are viewing pronounced tendencies for a late sensate culture, especially in the north-western European culture area in Protestant Europe – Britain, the Netherlands, north-west Germany, Scandinavia – and in Anglo-America and the Antipodes where the upper classes have a very pronounced tendency towards what critics would call nihilistic, cynical, and alienated forms of cultural expression and social behavior: drugs, pornography, vicarious violence, and a glorification in the perverse, the ugly and bizarre. It is, for example, very difficult to find a heroic painting or sculpture produced in the western world since the end of World War II. The high culture values dissidence, distortion and despair.

To a large degree, this is characteristic only of the high culture. The bulk of the population remains as traditional as ever. Modern art and music and literature are now more than 50 years old and yet have not gained popular acceptance. In the high culture, Freudian psychology is old-hat, yet is still considered silly or dirty

Messianic cults often symptomize faltering civilizations. In Auroville in Bengal a religion has sprouted from the teachings of mystic, Aurobindo (*d* 1950).

Founded in 1968, Auroville has a planned population of 50,000 making it the most ambitious of the many recent 'counter culture' communities.

The attraction of Auroville crosses all national boundaries. Disciples flock from all over the world, eager to join the new religious community.

The pressures and sense of alienation in Harlem's 'ghetto' breed a resentment which can turn any confrontation into an explosive, violent situation.

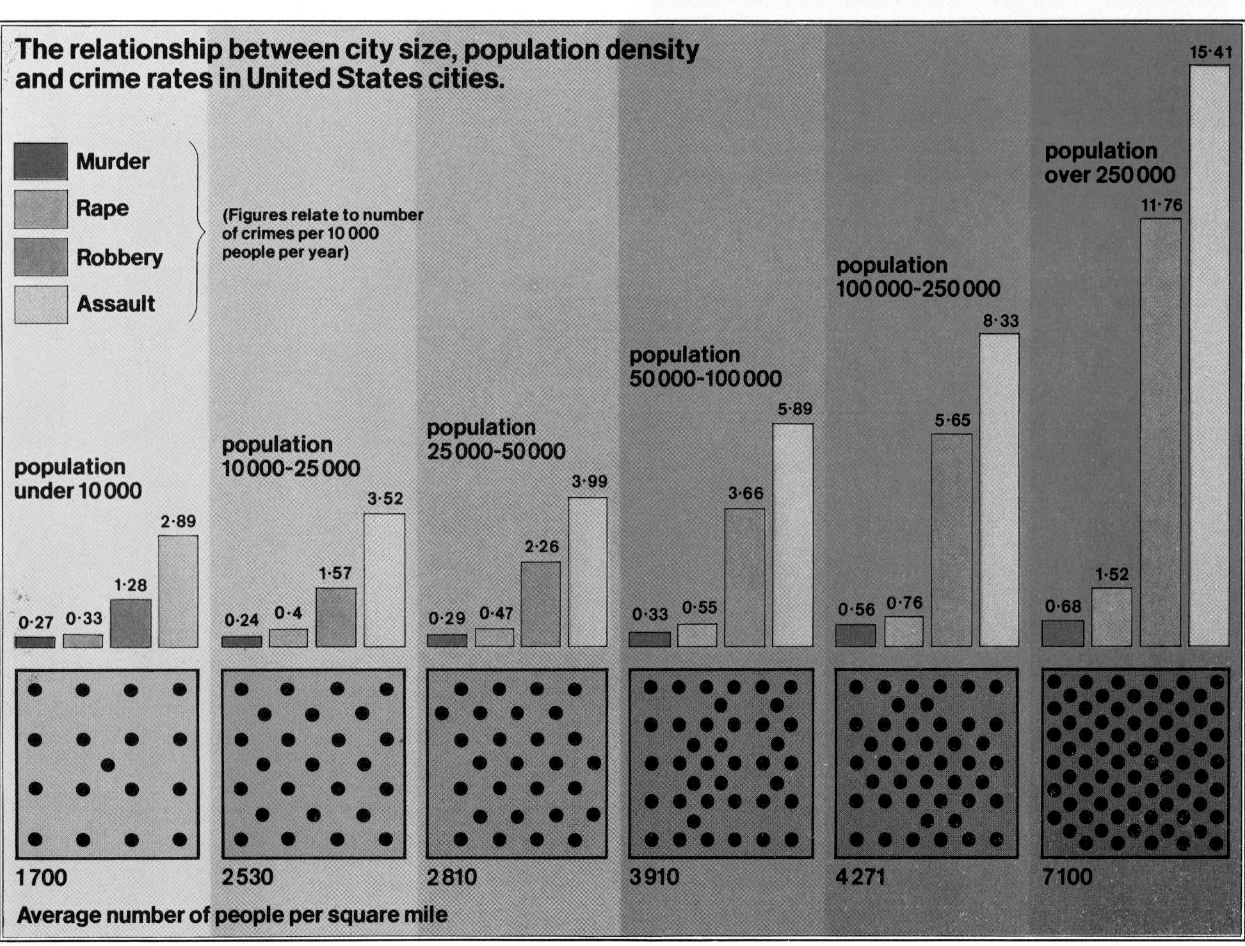

The Japanese are no exception in turning to violence as a way of evoking a positive response to their presence and wishes from an impersonal government.

by the masses. The more simplified and vulgarized types of modern architecture, furniture design, and industrial design, on the other hand, have filtered down and found wide acceptance among at least the middle classes in the western world. But the avant garde of the 20th century has generally not secured a following. This does not bode well for the future of high culture in the west. We seem to have been having grave difficulty producing great art of the quality which appeared in the period immediately after the World War II. As the Stravinskys, Picassos, and Faulkners die off no-one replaces them. It would appear highly likely that Oswald Spengler's prediction for western culture is coming to pass – that all that we can expect are new forms of nihilism and Alexandrian pastiches of previous themes. The best of these will be brilliant, entertaining and even elegant, but will lack originality and spiritual depth.

Another aspect of the long-term multifold trend is very important in its cultural manifestations. Increasingly the world is being run by bourgeois élites which under whatever nominal political or economic system seem to have a certain common cultural outlook. They have a taste for utilitarianism, for practicality, a rejection of the irrational, the traditional and colorful. This tendency varies from area to area. But towards the end of the century we may expect further the predominance in the western world of the progressive upper middle class, who owe their position in the world to education and their own efforts, rather than from family or possession of property. The feudal and martial values of honor, personal courage, loyalty, deference, and family allegiance should consequently be even further eroded.

The present and projected decay in high culture is accompanied by the rise of commercial pop culture. For

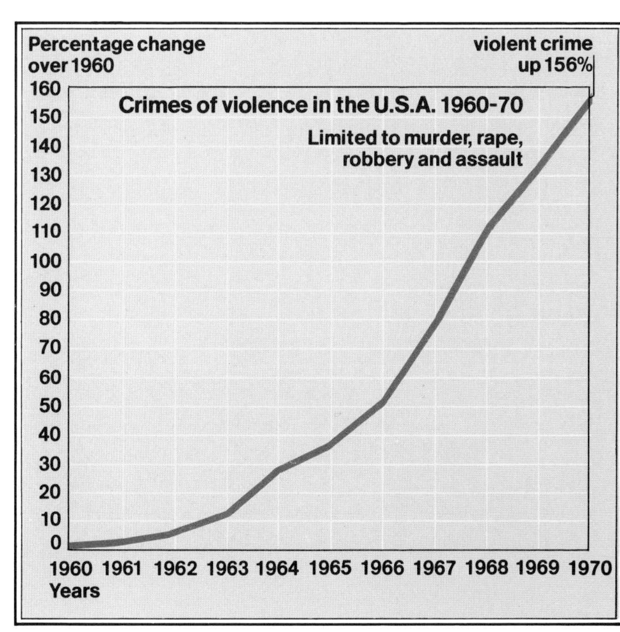

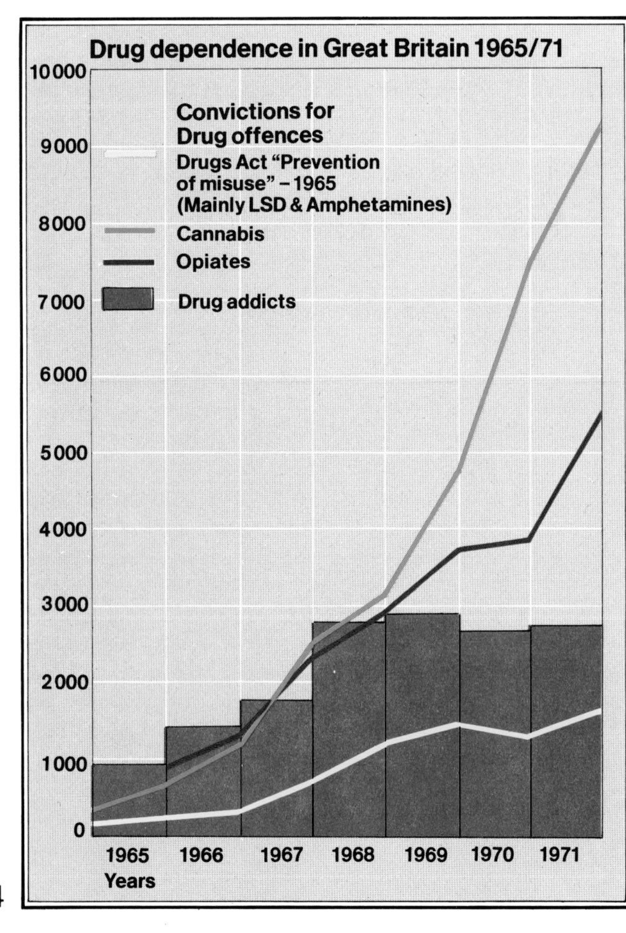

As crime grows, what will be the sanctions? Prisons like Attica, New York, fail to prevent crime and may increase it by acting as breeding grounds.

Experiments with 'open prisons' seek to teach prisoners new skills and give a sense of direction instead of reinforcing a negative attitude.

the first time since the beginning of the modern ages the broad masses of the industrial west dominate the cultural life of their society. The dominant figures of the culture are those entertainers, artists, and promoters who know how to cater to and, to some degree at least, shape the mass taste. By traditional standards most of this product may seem superficial, shallow and crude, yet even its most severe critics would find it hard to deny that it is vibrant and seemingly irresistible.

There is furthermore, a growing internationalization of western commercial culture. Indeed it has long since captured the imagination of the urban élites and is rapidly penetrating broader segments of the urban proletariat and the more prosperous classes in rural areas of non-western societies. It is becoming the world's first ecumenical culture. Its presence can even be felt in very austere socialist countries. The Warsaw Pact nations have nearly given up trying to resist this form of western decadence. New York, London, Paris, and Tokyo spread the latest fad, fashion and fancy to the rest of the world. Only the most austere and strong-willed rulers, as in Burma and mainland China, can protect their citizens from the inroads of pop culture.

Although the pop culture is increasingly international, its principal element is American and it remains true that its spread can rightly be called Americanization. North America was the first society in human history to establish a social system with broadly prosperous masses having the funds to invest in leisure and culture. The peculiar form of colonization moreover left North America effectively without a dominant class to impose its cultural values. America was the first democratic society and as de Tocqueville predicted early in the 19th century, was the first to create a democratic culture. Most of the very striking outward manifestations of contemporary consumer culture are American in nature – the mass use of the automobile, rock music, soft drinks, radio and television, and the devotion of serious intellectual effort toward commercial advertizing. The political and economic supremacy of the United States in the generation following World War II was certainly a powerful factor in contributing to its cultural hegemony. This unchallenged dominance may however be on the wane, along with the obvious erosion of US economic and political power as Europe, the Soviet Union and Japan reestablish something more nearly resembling a more balanced distribution of influence in the world.

Conservative projections of Japanese growth indicate that Japan will be the world's wealthiest society by the end of the century. Such economic prosperity means cultural puissance. Japan would have the same world position as England *circa* 1910 and America *circa* 1960. Within a generation Japan's leadership in consumer technology will be well established and the Japanese will have developed many new and exotic ways to spend money, particularly as they shed their present inferiority complex *vis-a-vis* the west. There could be a passion for things Japanese. We may already see a harbinger of this in the world-wide interest in Japanese martial arts. The samurai might have replaced the cowboy as the paladin of vicarious violence. Prefabricated Japanese-style houses and other products of the peculiarly Japanese mixture of a rice culture with post-industrialization would be commonplace snob goods. Cosmopolitan slang would likely include a smattering of Japanese.

A consequence of the failure of high culture and the flourishing of pop culture has been a general cultural leveling throughout the world. With few exceptions, societies had, until the beginning of the modern period, fairly uniform cultures. There was very little difference in the values and education of the rich and powerful, and the peasantry. The Renaissance began the division of society by means of formal education and led to the creation of what we think of as modern western culture. But the advent of mass education has led to a general blurring of lines and a strong tendency toward leveling. With each year there seems to be less and less difference between the rich, well-born, and well-bred on the one hand and the herd on the other.

Tendencies toward cultural leveling are accelerated by a recent but fascinating phenomenon among the upper classes in the west. Very substantial segments of the privileged orders are rejecting their cultural heritage and eagerly embracing the cultural manifestations of the lower classes. This can be called proletarianization. Its most obvious aspect is the embrace of rock music and drugs and the glorification of rock stars and other folk heroes by the most plush salons and the adaptation of lower class dress by children of the élite. The proletarianization of manners is equally obvious.

Perhaps some of the above trends seem contradictory. No doubt. But over the next few generations we will probably have to forget about having a unitary culture; the only real solution to these contradictions in anything resembling a free society will be a mosaic society wherein a number of value systems and life-styles coexist. But we can expect continued cultural malaise. The world of the late 20th century could in many ways resemble the last pagan centuries when there were similar searches for meaning and purpose. Much as Hellenistic Greek and Roman culture consolidated Hellenic culture we might have a westernistic civilization built on western culture, expanding its material horizons but lacking its spiritual content. As in the Hellenistic age, this society could be characterized by a wide-spread sense of its civilization being the culmination of history by a style of decadence, by monumental but not heroic architecture, and by huge work projects (great transport systems, space exploration), which will be an exciting fulfilment of modern technology but will probably be viewed by the most highly cultured élites with a sense of *ennui* or even contempt.

Churches stand empty or are sold as interest in conventional religion declines while the need for religion remains, sending searchers eastward.

Third world city

A major socio-economic crisis which threatens to engulf most of the tropical world has been gathering since the middle of the 20th century. Many demographers and ecologists believe that the breakdown point will have been reached before the year 2000. Throughout the continents or subcontinents of Latin America, southern Asia and Africa, the population of the great cities is growing at a rapid pace. While it is generally known that the population of the world will have doubled by the end of the century, fewer people appreciate that by then half of mankind will be urbanized. Of this exploding urban population – leaping ahead twice as fast as the total population – the greater part belongs to the third world.

Here the city populations are rising at three times the rate at which European cities grew in the 19th century. Already in Latin America more than half the inhabitants have become urbanized. In Argentina alone 7·5 million of the total population of 25 million live in the single conurbation of Buenos Aires. Before the end of the century, Calcutta's inhabitants will number more than 60 million. Even in the relatively underpopulated vastness of Africa over 15 per cent of the inhabitants are urbanized. Overall, cities in the third world are doubling their populations every 10-15 years. Of course, the majority of people in these countries (with the exception of Latin America) still live in rural areas and depend overwhelmingly on agriculture for their existence, but if the European pattern of urbanization is repeated, then very soon, given the much faster pace of city-expansion in the third world, 70-80 per cent of the people in these areas will end up city-dwellers. Toynbee's concept of a 'world city' is not that far off realization.

Hong Kong's teeming poor cram into cheap high-rise flats and shanty dwellings. Immigration and a high birth-rate are typical of tropical cities.

The most obvious indicators of this untoward growth in tropical cities are the shanty towns, *bidonvilles* or *villes extra-coutumiers*. Whatever the local variation in description, the reality for the dweller in these slums is depressingly standard throughout the third world. Every great city in the tropics (and even in Europe, for example Paris) has these quarters, where shacks and every kind of improvised shelter have been thrown together on the outskirts of the city by the migrants from the countryside or the dispossessed urban-born. These pathetic dwellings coexist with the skyscrapers, factories and other modern buildings of the rich city and foreign business élites. In the shanty towns, where the poor dream of making a successful living from employment in the city basic amenities are nil, hunger and disease rife. Yet an increasing proportion of tropical city dwellers is forced to subsist in these conditions. Half of Ankara's populace, a third of Mexico City's, half of Kinshasa's, live in makeshift dwellings. Hundreds of thousands of Calcutta's inhabitants live and die on the pavements. Of Kanpur's 1.5 million population, 30,000 have the pavements as their only dwellings. In Latin America 40 million people are squatters.

Much of the increase in tropical city populations results from the influx of people from the countryside into the towns. Despite the poor opportunities for employment and decent habitation, peasants flock into the cities at a rate which helps to double the normal increase in their populations. A few people migrate because, whatever the apparent disadvantages, the prospects of city life seem to offer more opportunities. The majority, however, migrate because they have no alternative. In most of the countries of the third world the rural areas are stagnating. Feudal or quasi-feudal land tenure systems inhibit development. The terms of trade between the industrial nations and the developing nations do nothing to encourage this in any case – the upward trend in agricultural prices still does not generate much capital for investment. Moreover the trading links between the developed and underdeveloped world often work to the latter's disadvantage – the poor nations sell their agricultural produce in exchange for capital-intensive machinery which increases unemployment and underemployment in the countryside, as well as draining their capital resources.

All this drives people from rural to urban areas. Another factor which swells the city populations is natural increase. Contrary to western experience urban-

Caracas *barrios* show lack of opportunity for the floods of rural migrants. Venezuela's oil-rich, US-backed government has managed few improvements.

ization in the tropical world has been accompanied by lower death rates than in the countryside. This is a result of the improved technology of death control over 19th-century Europe. Urban fertility rates in tropical cities are also about the same as rural fertility rates, not lower as in the western experience. Hence the growth of population from natural increase is almost as important a factor as rural-urban migration. This means that in many cases it is not urbanization that is necessarily the key factor in any given country, but city growth. Such a distinction takes on more significance when the role of the city in economic development and structural changes in society are considered.

Industrialization in Europe followed a well-defined pattern. Modernization in the countryside was followed by a sharp rise in agricultural production and an increasing trading surplus which made the accumulation of capital and investment in industry possible. Two or three times as many people were employed by industry as lived in towns or cities. In Latin America at present, three or four times as many people live in urban areas as are engaged in industry. The western nations were able to expand their field of activities to accommodate their spreading economies and increasing populations. Although the tropical cities have a nucleus of what looks like a modern, national, progressive, industrial center, with a burgeoning middle class in fact these are mere extensions of the western economic system. Foreign capital predominates; domestic capital, if it exists, has little chance against the vast multinational conglomerates. The westernized sector of the cities usually coexists with a bazaar-type sector, which has links both with the modern sector and with the rural hinterland. Change comes to the cities, but the peasant system of exchange still continues to operate among the vast proportion of its inhabitants. New attitudes and aspirations are superimposed on to an age-old style of living and do not represent economic growth or structural change. There are few self-inspired alternatives in this atmosphere, and real growth is limited by the near-saturation point reached by most markets throughout the world.

What happens in tropical cities in the last quarter of the century will therefore reflect the general problems of underdevelopment. Whether these cities are convulsed with social upheavals or not depends largely on how well the problems of economic development are tackled. And this depends on the attitude of the developed world.

Another threat to the well-being of the tropical cities is man's simple preference for membership of a small group. As the American biologist, René Dubos, has pointed out, since the beginning of human life on this planet, the vast majority of people have spent their entire lives in such groups. This pattern of behavior persisted through the centuries and it is unreasonable to suppose that this pattern will become less valid in a massively urbanized and industrialized world.

Threatened peoples

Tribal minorities, who live at the opposite end of the philosophical spectrum from technological man, face extinction by the end of this century. The threat to their existence comes not only from direct attacks involving murder, enslavement, disease and dispossession of their lands but, at an increasing rate, from economic exploitation, surrounding population pressures and the demoralizing effect of being regarded as 'backward' and a barrier to progress. Yet, as we have seen in the other volumes in this series, their life style is often superior to that of the developed world and their values more tenable and enduring. At a time when industrial societies are beginning to question their own value systems much concern is being expressed over diminishing resources and there is a growing awareness that, in spite of all our technical advances, the quality of life for the majority of the world's population appears to be deteriorating rather than improving. It is timely to consider what the future holds for those belonging to alternative societies and what lessons can be learnt from them.

Most of the tribal societies which survive today live in the relatively undisturbed habitats of the tropics – the richest, most varied and potentially the most productive areas on this planet. Since all development inevitably involves destruction it is essential that we consider carefully how we should best set about developing these regions so that the maximum benefit accrues to all and the potential of the tropics is not squandered. If we are to avoid the mistakes of the past, the creation of deserts and dust bowls, scrub land and sterile waste, then it is vital that we face the implications of our actions and bring every available source of knowledge to bear on the problem. At the moment the often senseless rape of the tropics is accelerating. Untold areas of jungle are cut down without re-afforestation programs. Huge tracts of fertile land are flooded in hydro-electric schemes. Swamps, estuaries and wet lands – the breeding grounds of innumerable species of fish – are drained, polluted or deprived of their water supply.

One source of knowledge that has been almost totally ignored is the accumulated experience of those peoples who have lived most intimately with the regions that are being destroyed. For thousands of years they have experimented with their environment, learning the value of each plant and animal and creating perfectly viable and, until recently, durable societies. Although our own knowledge and needs have taken us beyond the point where we can hope to emulate these people it is surely foolhardy not to learn from them and at the same time attempt not to eliminate them.

The most publicized and, at present probably the most threatened, tribal peoples in the world are the lowland Indians of South America. In Brazil alone a population which numbered between three and five million Indians in 1500 when the Portuguese Cabral first set foot on the coast has been reduced to 50,000 to 80,000 today. The

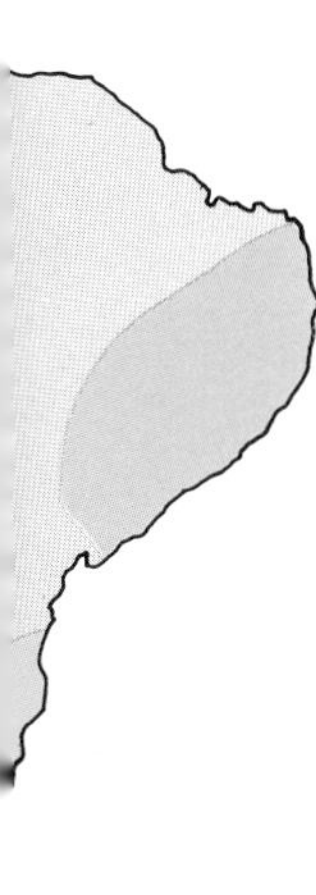

The lowland tribes of South America are probably the most threatened peoples of the world.

The smallest tribes are numbered on the map in red: 1 Tetetes 2 Araona 3 Pacaguara 4 Cayuvava 5 Jora 6 Canichana 7 Pauserna 8 Chane 9 Xeta 10 Guato 11 Manitsawa 12 Anambe 13 Juma 14 Awake 15 Sape. These tribes each number less than 40 individuals and all or most of them will be extinct in the near future. The Tetetes of Ecuador, for example, probably number no more than 3 people. The Jora of Bolivia are only 8 in number and the Xeta of Brazil are 5 or 6.

The largest tribal groups – numbered on the map in green – range from about 6,000 to about 50,000: 1 Guajiro 2 Catio 3 Paez 4 Guahibo 5 Quichuas 6 Shuar 7 Aguaruna 8 Cocama 9 Ticuna 10 Shipibo 11 Campa 12 Chiquitano 13 Chiriguano 14 Toba 15 Terena. Whilst there is a certain amount of linguistic, cultural or social affiliation within each group some sub-divisions of the group may not necessarily consider themselves members of the same group. The size of these tribes makes it unlikely that they are faced with a direct threat of extinction – although some sub-divisions of the groups may be.

Between these two extremes there are many, quite large, isolated tribal groups, such as the Macusa of Colombia, and the Kreen Akrore of Brazil who will come into direct contact with 'white' society over the next few years. The future of these tribes depends on the action taken when this contact takes place.

There are groups, such as the Ache of Paraguay who, although they still number a few hundred, are being treated in such a brutal way that unless immediate action is taken to ensure their survival, stand little or no chance of existing after the 1980s. Another group facing depletion is the Cuna of Panama who live on a reservation in the Bayamo river area. Eighty per cent of this reservation is due to be flooded on the completion of the Bayamo river dam project.

Brazilian government vacillates between referring to them as 'ethnic cysts' and hailing the Villas Boas brothers, who have worked in their defense for 30 years, as national heroes. In the Xingu National Park, which the Villas Boas brothers created, live 15 tribes who are here protected from the shocks and pressures endured by their neighbors and given time to come to terms with what is happening. There, almost alone in Brazil, the Indian population is slowly increasing and, in spite of a road being cut through their land, demoralization has not set in. Elsewhere, although many civil servants, missionaries and doctors have worked strenuously to help the Indians, the picture has all too often been one of decimation through disease and aggression, leaving a remnant population of beggars.

In other parts of South America the situation is no better. Corruption and a deliberate desire to remove or enslave the Indians have usually resulted in the degeneration of once strong societies into social problems which are a financial burden to the country, an embarrassment to foreign relations and breeding grounds of political unrest. In Colombia recently a group of settlers was acquitted from a charge of murdering 16 Cuiva Indians on the grounds that they had not realized the Indians were human beings. Following, and in part due to, international protest they were re-tried.

In Africa centuries of slavery and colonial influence, first by the Arabs and later by the European powers, have permanently changed the way of life and aspirations of the vast majority of the people so that the few remaining nomads and hunter-gatherers have been forced onto the poorest desert and waste land. Of the Bushmen, who once roamed over the whole continent, only a handful now survive in the Kalahari desert and the swamps of Botswana.

Recent events in Indo-China have brought another form of culture shock. Where the succession of wars in and around Vietnam and the associated guerilla fighting have brought sophisticated modern warfare such as mass defoliation and napalm bombing to the villages of even the remotest peoples living in the highlands and jungles. The effect of these, as well as of the accompanying intense psychological and political pressures, can as yet only be imagined. But it is clear that the unfortunate tribes caught up in the frenzied and, to them at least, incomprehensible activities taking place around them, have suffered appallingly and are unlikely ever to readjust.

Guerilla warfare and internal strife have affected tribal peoples regarded as a threat to national security throughout South-east Asia. These peoples are sometimes unwittingly caught up in political battles as useful fighters for both sides and suffer inevitable retribution when one side wins. In Burma, Thailand and Malaya this has been a familiar picture since the Japanese occupation. In Borneo the British, the Communists and the Indonesians all used Dayak tribes in this way.

The Tasaday were discovered in an isolated valley of the Philippines in 1971. The recent Muslim rebellion has hampered efforts for tribal protection.

In Indonesia, where there are about half a million officially classified 'isolated peoples', the pressures are somewhat different. Since the Japanese occupation of World War II, and since independence and the attempted Communist coup of 1965 the country has begun rapid economic development. This has involved granting large concessions to foreign companies to exploit the country's mineral and forestry resources. Previously remote, little-visited regions have suddenly been opened up. Camps have been built employing large numbers of foreign male workers. Disease, alcohol and foreign goods as well as prostitution and forced labor have been introduced as a result. Even well-intentioned laws, such as the rule designed to protect the smaller trees, that only hardwood trees of over 60 centimeters in diameter may be cut, have sometimes worked against the interests of the indigenous inhabitants. Lacking the chain saws and tractors needed to extract these forest giants many of the local people have found themselves deprived of their only cash crop. They are even less able than they might have been to afford the flood of commodities suddenly available in the trade stores and coastal villages. The gap between them and the rest of society is widened and, combined with the ardent desire on the part of the government to 'civilize' them, demoralization follows. In many areas inland tribes are migrating to the coast where most of the towns are. The police find them easier to administer in settlements. The tribes leave the rich interior empty, lose their skills and die of boredom.

The Melanesians of New Guinea and of the many surrounding smaller islands, live in a wide variety of environments and represent an amazing diversity of cultures and languages. Through their long tradition of trading and acquiring wealth they stand a better chance of coming to terms with the pressures of the modern world. Their insatiable curiosity for new things and their willingness to accept change is in marked contrast to the Aborigines of Australia and indeed to the Amerindians and Bushmen whose cultures are more fragile and easily shocked. Nonetheless they have suffered from the shock of sudden change and the prohibition of such customs as ritual warfare. They are consequently beset by many problems and traumas, as witnessed by the proliferation of cargo cults. Attempting to rationalize the sudden arrival of dazzling quantities of western commodities which they had no money to buy, which came in airplanes and giant ships which they had not the skills to build, they came to hold the white man's strong magic responsible. As a result many people followed leaders who prophesied that if all the old ways were abandoned and the trappings of civilization adopted – such as European clothes, mock radio aerials and even crude airstrips –

The Bushmen – an ancient negroid people – once roamed the whole of Africa. Now only a few survive in the remote Kalahari desert.

then it would only be a matter of waiting until the promised goods arrived. During the war an occasional aircraft did crash and ships were wrecked, adding fuel to the myth. Meanwhile gardens were left untended, ceremonial objects burnt, and established systems forgotten. No instant new way of life replaced them.

From the Eskimo to the Amerindians and from the Bushmen to the Tasaday, people once isolated by their environment, their way of life or their very remoteness from other members of the human race find themselves today beset by change as their land is taken from them and their traditions attacked. Many are alive today because they have rejected change and chosen to flee deeper into shrinking uninhabited areas. Others have welcomed progress but failed to come to terms with it. Preserving them like flies in amber, insulated from all outside pressures and dangers, is usually no longer practical nor desirable. But rapid change has nearly always left them worse off than before. Like all mankind, respect and understanding is what they need, with the time to adjust to a new and confusing set of circumstances.

These are said to be the doomed peoples of the world: tribal societies whose cultural and physical survival is threatened by the manifestations of a technological and progressive world. A few years ago there seemed little hope for them. The rate at which they were disappearing was accelerating and, while concern for wild life, wilderness areas and other vital components of our planet's ecosystem was growing, the peoples who continued to live most closely in harmony with their environment appeared to have little to expect from the future except a similar extinction or, if they were able to withstand the shock of the process, grudging acceptance into the very lowest strata of a society which despised them and forced them to live as beggars and menial workers.

This process continues. But recently there have been signs that, at the last moment, the world is waking up to the problem. Something may be done before it is too late. As with all things that become rare, their very rarity stimulates interest. This series of books is an example of people's growing interest in 'different' peoples and their needs. Organizations to help the threatened peoples in their struggle for survival have been set up in many countries, both in the western world where most such peoples have already vanished or have been (usually brutally) assimilated, and also in the developing countries where most of these peoples still exist. Some governments are beginning to take action to protect their tribal minorities.

Perhaps before it is too late we may learn to share the world with peoples whose values and traditions differ from our own but whose knowledge and awareness of it is no less intimate. If this can come about without paternalism on the one hand or squalid degeneration on the other, the world will be a better place to live in.

The Kamayurá Indians in the Xingu National Park, Brazil, are one of the 15 tribes who are increasing unlike other South American Indians.

Man and medicine

By the year 2000 mankind will be well on its way towards realizing the age-old dream of freeing itself from disease. The two most important steps along this road are overdue. They are health education and health motivation.

People are appallingly ill-informed about what is good and what is harmful to them. In the next decade they will learn that malnutrition is not just a function of poverty: an adequate diet need cost no more and often costs less than the time-hallowed eating habits by which people are preventing themselves and their children from reaching full health. In poor countries that will mean making better-balanced foods and food additives available and educating people to accept them. For the rich it means learning the dangers of overeating and indulgence in alcohol, smoking, barbiturates and other regularly used drugs. The vast majority of rich and poor people need more than their diet provides of at least one, usually several, vitamins and trace elements. A tremendous task lies ahead just teaching humanity how to eat.

Parents tend to be woefully ignorant about child care. For instance tens of millions of babies are permanently impaired in their mental development each year, not only by lack of essential nutrients, but as importantly by lack of the minimum stimulation which is indispensable for reaching full human potential. Even the infant in the crib needs sights, sounds, human contact and response. The earlier parents learn such things, the fewer subnormal humans will be a burden to themselves and to society.

Health education cannot rest content to tell people what is needed for good health; it must motivate them to do it. We have been surprisingly unsuccessful in this respect. A large majority let their teeth and gums decay, knowing full well that a visit to the dentist could save them. Although the treatment is known to be simple, effective and usually free of charge, millions leave their venereal disease untreated at great damage to themselves and at great risk to those they continue to infect.

Once people are motivated to report for regular checkups, cheap, fast and accurate early diagnosis becomes crucial. Even though some of today's instruments can automatically and simultaneously perform as many as 16 different diagnostic tests on a few drops of blood or urine, the tests we can interpret are but a minute fraction of the millions of potentially diagnostic tests and measurements that could be developed.

In keeping track of millions of measurements of variables and interpreting their significance, medicine is about to acquire an invaluable ally, the computer. By the year 2000 computers will assist in taking medical histories, ordering batteries of automated tests, and will keep permanent records of results. This means not only that the individual's record is immediately retrievable at any medical center. It also means that test measurements are available for hundreds of millions of humans in correlation with each other and with the sex, race, date

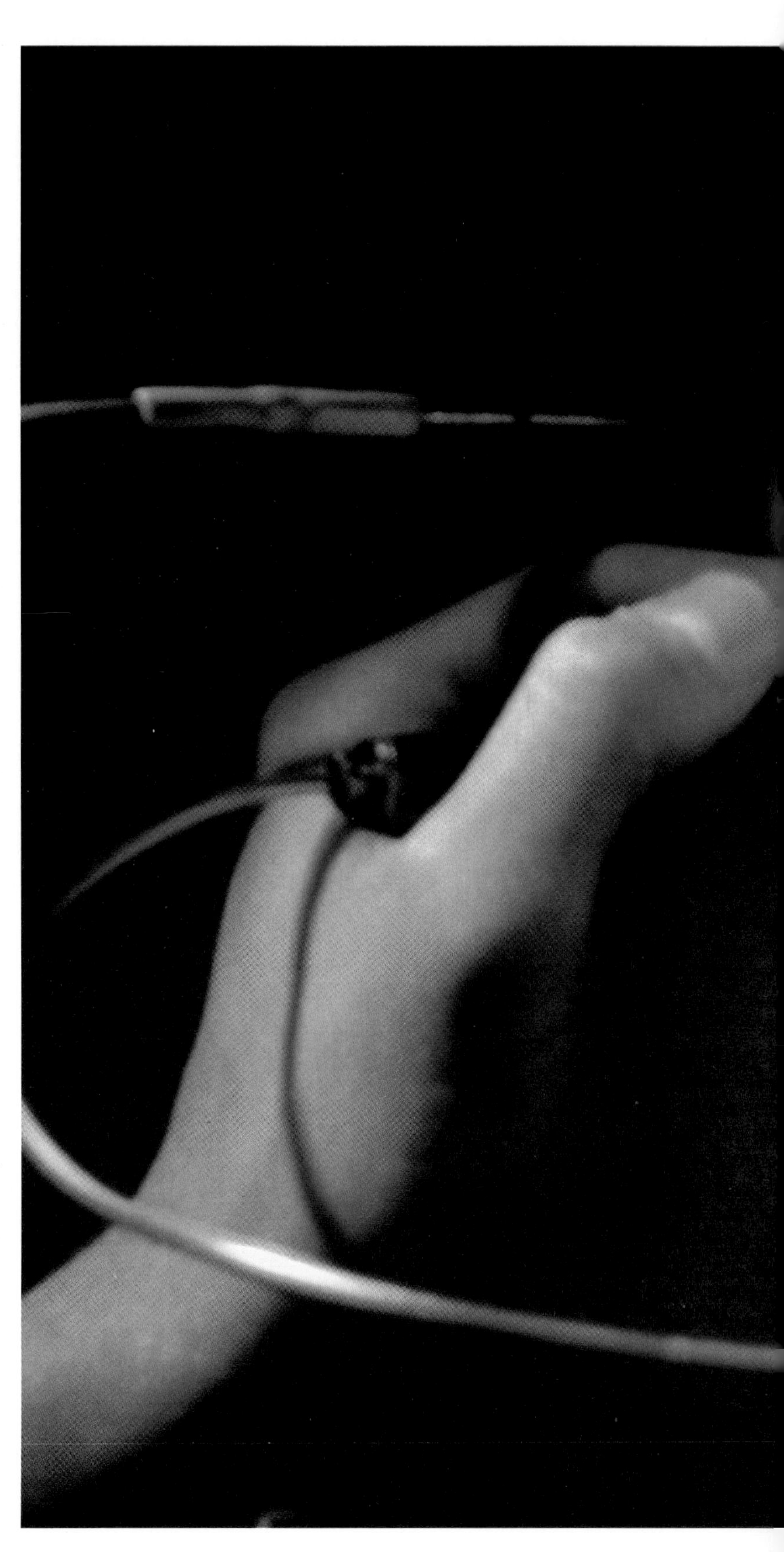

A ten-week old human fetus can be kept alive in this artificial womb for only 24 hours. Research may one day make artificial 'birth' possible.

Techniques of transplant surgery have been successful with kidneys and livers. Heart transplants, however, present greater problems of rejection.

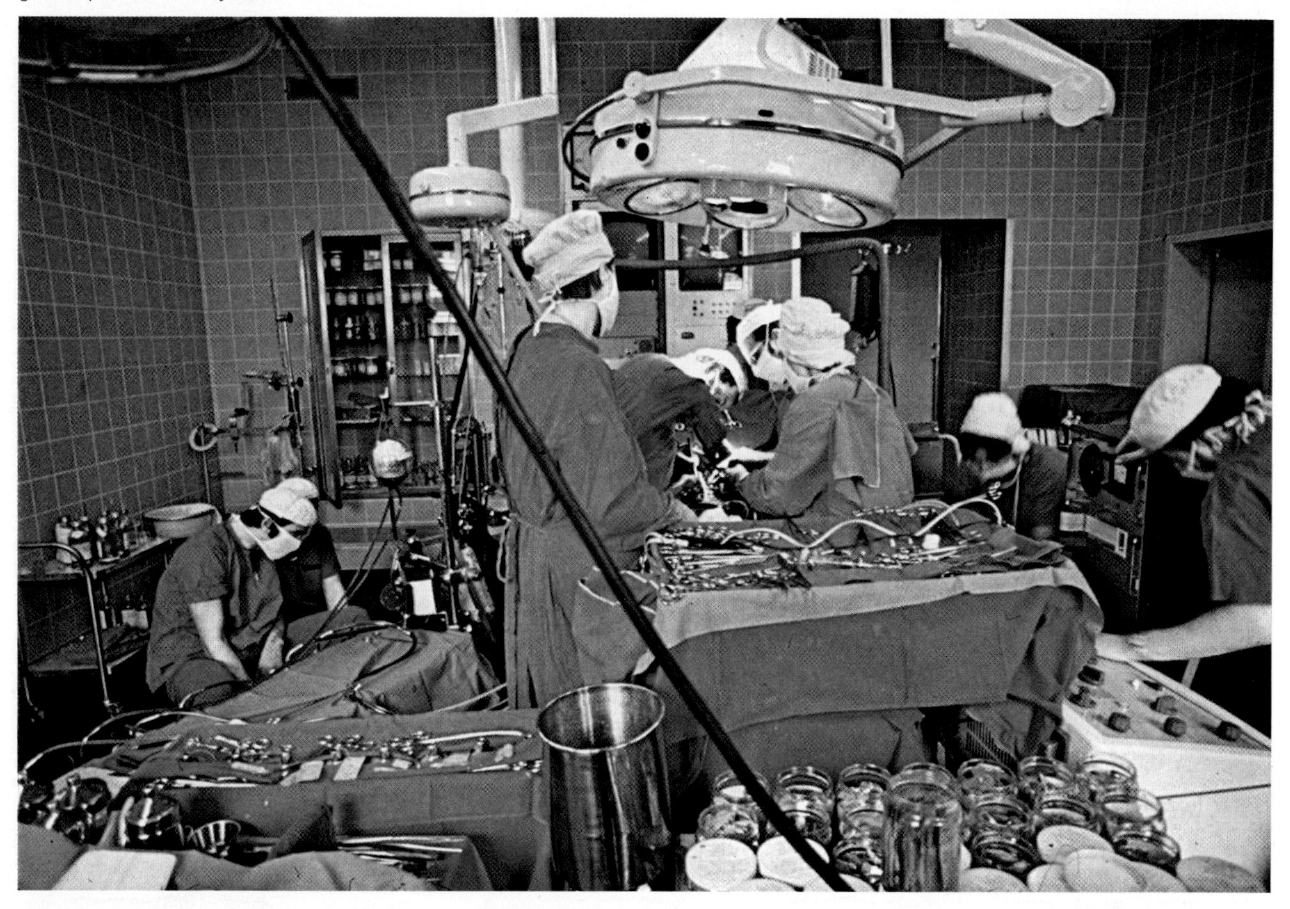

and place of birth, domicile, parentage, children and medical history of each of them. This will enormously broaden medical knowledge and understanding of the diagnostic significance of test data and will in turn contribute to more reliable diagnosis and prognosis of each individual patient's condition. Where the data could conceivably support more than one diagnosis, the computer itself will generate questions or order tests to differentiate between the alternatives. Uneliminated possibilities will each be listed on a computer printout with a probability figure to guide the physician in his final determination, which then becomes part of the record.

Diagnoses will be far more sophisticated than they are today. Instead of just pinpointing the cause of the overt symptoms a patient presents, the computer will be programmed to detect any deviations from a normal range in the history and in the test data and to signal possible threats to health from diet, environment, toxicants, undue stress or developing disease. Treatment will be predominantly prophylactic: instead of letting disease develop, preventive steps will be taken beforehand.

We shall not be content with timely treatment: humanity's aim will be nothing less than the total eradication of disease. With communicable diseases we are well on our way, by means of a triple line of attack.

The first line is prevention, which can take many forms. Perhaps the most successful of these has been immunization, which has almost eliminated smallpox, diphtheria and poliomyelitis. Public health measures to safeguard drinking water and food handling have made cholera and typhoid a rare occurrence in developed countries and will totally eliminate them from all countries in the next 20 years. Another public health activity, vector control, is effective in eliminating diseases carried to many by animal hosts (vectors). These include malaria, yellow fever, trachoma, typhus, rabies, plague.

The second line of attack is chemotherapy with synthetic drugs and antibiotics. A majority of bacterial infections has already been stemmed in this way; the rest will be brought under control in the next couple of decades, provided only that all infected people can be motivated to present themselves for treatment.

The third line of attack is a fast-developing new branch of science called molecular biology. It delves into the detailed structures which are responsible for the characteristics of viruses, cancer cells, protein synthesis, the immunity mechanisms, cell multiplication and heredity. The eradication of infection will be aided by such contributions of molecular biology as inhibiting multiplication

Biological engineers have created a cadaver 'man' of transplanted organs, including a heart, lungs, liver, bones, veins and eye corneas.

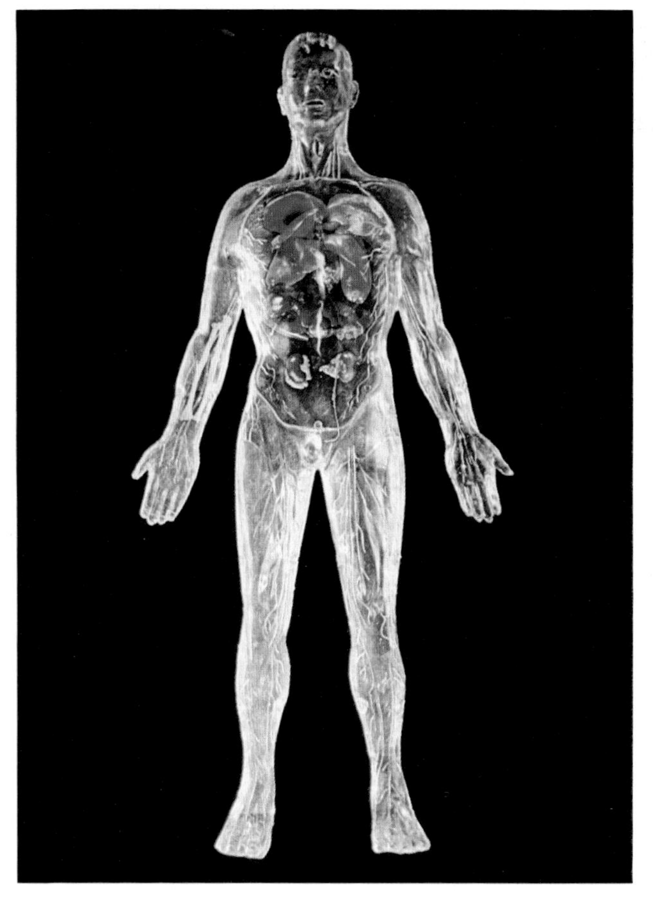

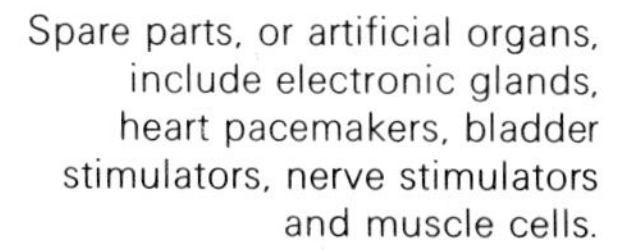

Spare parts, or artificial organs, include electronic glands, heart pacemakers, bladder stimulators, nerve stimulators and muscle cells.

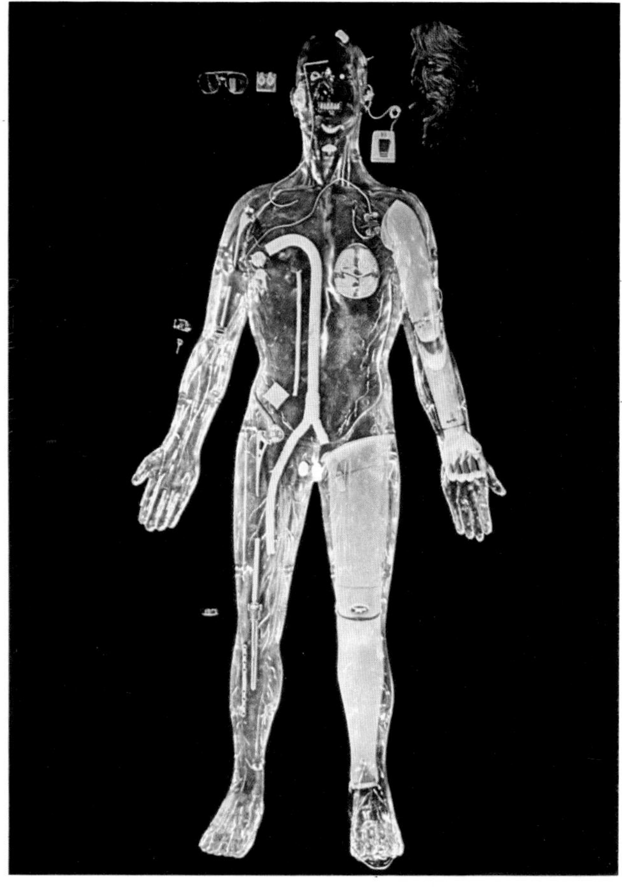

of pathogens; mobilizing the immunity mechanism against pathogens; using knowledge of the virus to destroy it; using harmless viruses against pathogenic viruses; using viruses to destroy bacteria.

The specter of cancer is also about to be exorcised forever. One of the many approaches of molecular biology may well play the decisive role. There is a connection between at least some cancers and viruses – protection against the virus might eliminate the risk of cancer. All cancers have peculiar methods of multiplication: their better understanding may give medicine the power to inhibit them. Many humans seem to possess natural immunity against the invasion of their body by cancer cells – if it were possible to call forth this immunity in cancer patients, the cancer would wither.

A concerted attack on serious inherited diseases has already begun. One method lies in the detection of potential parents who carry a genotypic defect that affects them little, but can be passed on to their children. Genetic counseling can then avoid a union liable to produce affected offspring or, in serious cases, avoid reproduction altogether, until a means can be found to repair or 'cure' the defective gene with the tools of molecular biology. More and more cures of this sort will continue to become feasible during the next 15 to 30 years. It is already possible to determine if the defect has been passed on to the unborn child. It may then be mitigated by timely treatment; otherwise interruption of the pregnancy may be indicated at this early stage. In time it will be possible to eliminate all heritable mental and physical disease from humanity's gene pool.

The greatest medical breakthrough of this century will be a safe, convenient, aesthetic and low-priced means of birth control. Ideally, that will be one a woman can receive once and then forget about until she actually desires to have a child, when it can easily be inactivated long enough to permit a pregnancy. Such a device or drug will be available in the early 1980s to a few and in the 1990s to all who want it. Experience has shown that, irrespective of their religious and cultural backgrounds, women tend to use means to regulate their fertility as long as these are not inconvenient or expensive.

Before 2000 means will also be widely available to determine the sex of one's child in advance, not only in the sense of predicting, but of actually selecting. The provision of a complete life support environment for embryonic development from zygote to new-born or, 'test tube' babies, is a challenging technical problem, but the reluctance to engage in this kind of experimentation persists because of ethical and legal considerations.

When extra-uterine techniques have been perfected, it will eventually be possible to grow whole human beings from other body cells, not necessarily only from a fertilized egg. Since each cell possesses the total genetic complement one could prepare a large number of exact genetic copies of a given individual. This process is called cloning. All the members of a clone would resemble each other as closely as identical twins. It would thus be possible to produce replicas of people with outstanding skills and create, for instance, a symphony orchestra or corps de ballet composed entirely of great virtuosi.

Tendency towards depression or schizophrenia seems to be due to a biochemical abnormality which will be detected and successfully treated with drugs. To the extent that the abnormality is inherited it may also be controlled genetically. So, undoubtedly, will mental deficiencies caused by genetic error. Mental aberrations caused by stress will decrease as a result of eugenic, nutritional and educational improvements. Ugliness and deformity are already getting rarer and, when they still occur, can often be surgically repaired.

The best way of preventing humans from succumbing to the stress of frustration or to the burdens of responsibility is to bring them up from childhood to handle both occasional frustrations and regular responsibilities. Treatment of the symptoms of neurosis is both quicker and more successful than a long quest for the postulated root causes. By the year 2000, psychoanalysis as therapy will be extinct. But the psychiatrist will have a powerful armamentarium to overcome aberrative behavior.

A patient can be taught to regain control of himself by recognizing when it begins to slip. In one such technique an electric device is triggered by the early physiological signals accompanying the undesired behavior. For instance, the slight sweating preceding a fit of rage can be picked up by an instrument which by a noise or an electric shock warns the patient that he must reassert control over his sympathetic nervous system.

Until now there has been relatively little scientific research into powerful mind-affecting drugs, but their time has come and their possibilities are virtually unlimited. By the end of this century, psychiatrists will be able to administer drugs to control aberrative mental states: not only anxiety and tension but also guilt, fear, wrath and shock. Drugs will produce either mental alertness or relaxation at will; or enhance learning ability and memory, or dull or even suspend them temporarily.

The horror of electro-shock and prefrontal lobotomy will soon be a thing of the past. But the work on electric stimulation of the brain (ESB) may be used at the end of the century for a few conditions which do not respond equally fast or selectively to drugs. The present technique requires implantation of electrodes in a specific area of the brain which can then be stimulated as needed by the psychiatrist, by an automatic control device or by the patient himself (this last technique is also called intra-

A way of 'seeing' for the blind – a camera converts an image to a pattern of dots which then vibrate on the patient's back.

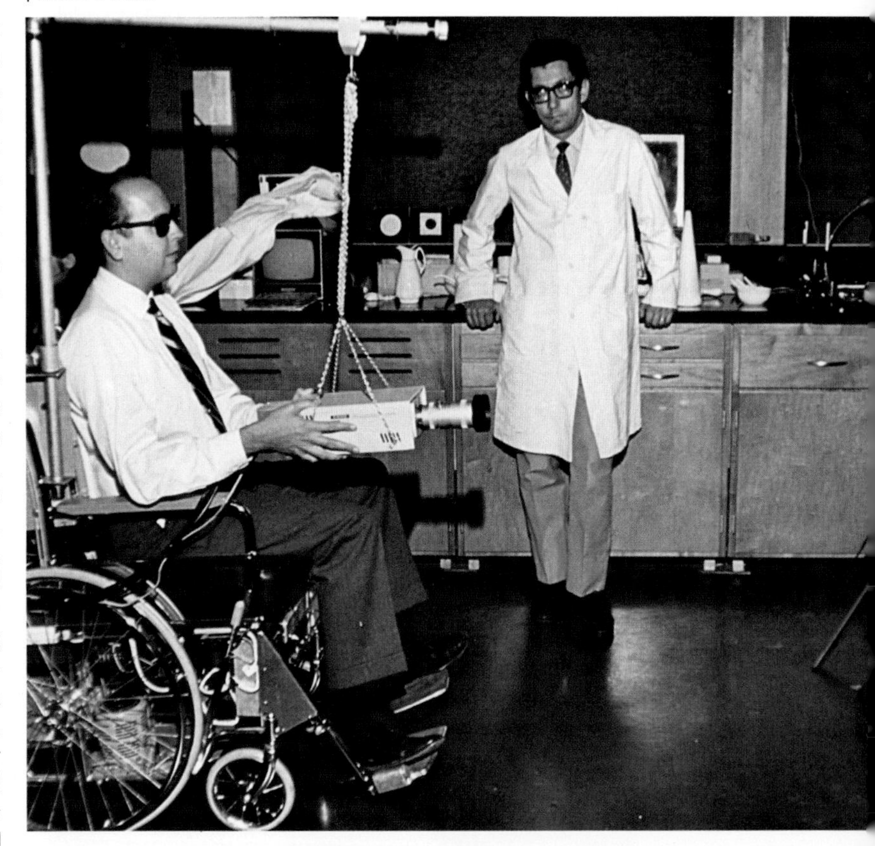

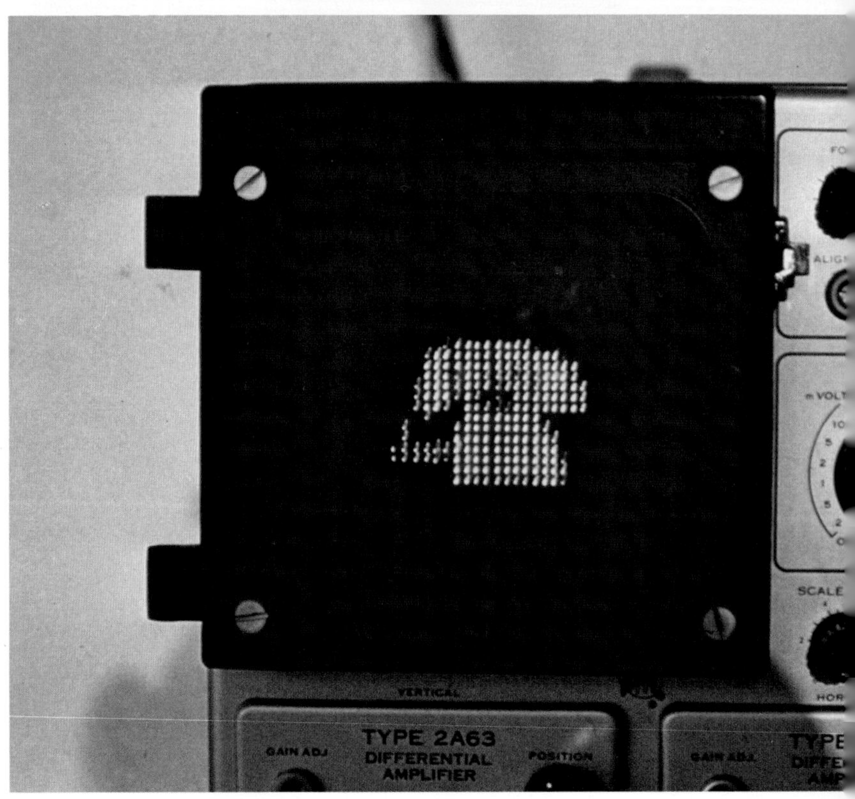

Dots make up the image of a telephone. A refined system like this might be linked up directly with the visual center of the brain.

An electronic current is passed to electrodes planted in a monkey's brain, making one arm move – in fact reproducing an order from the brain.

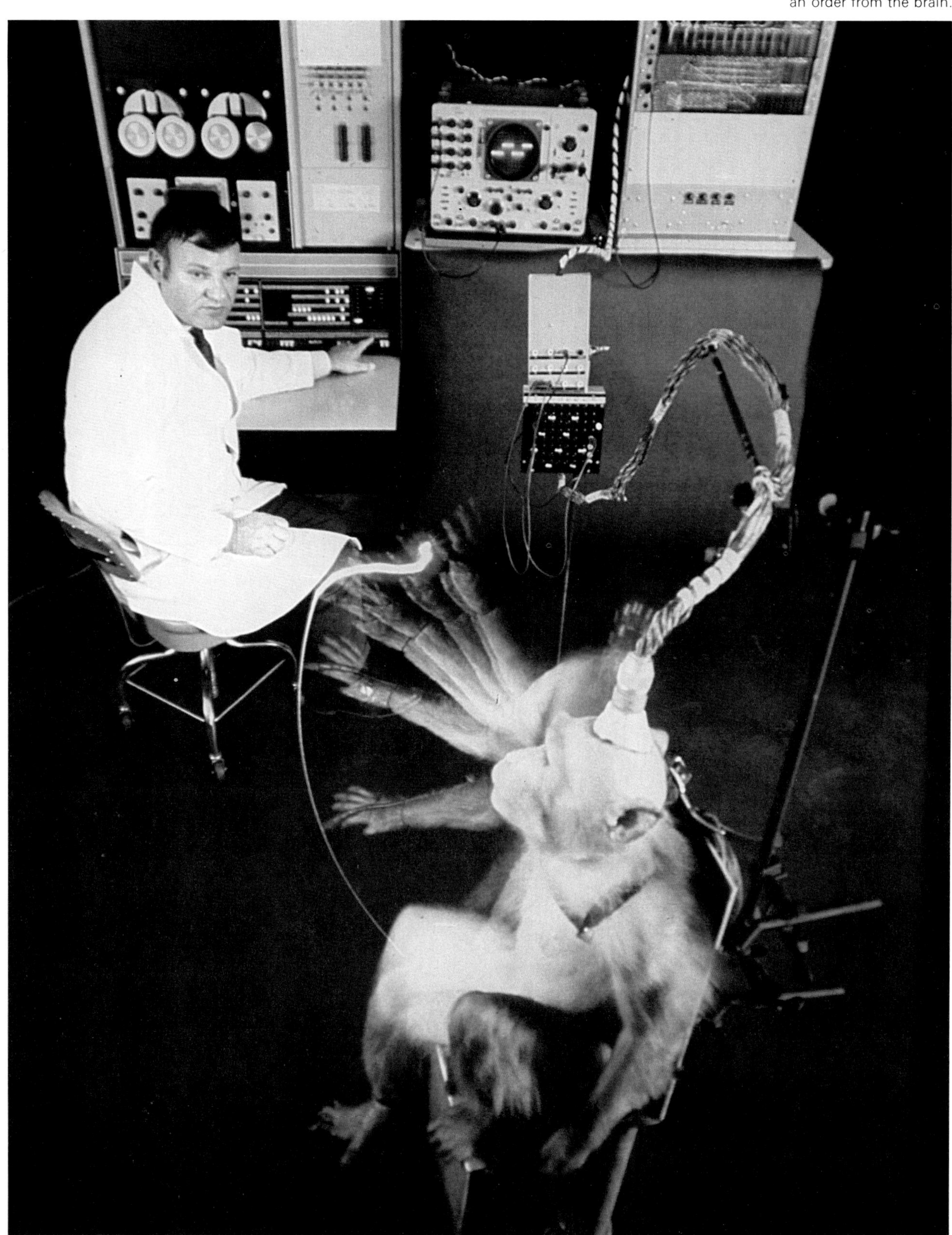

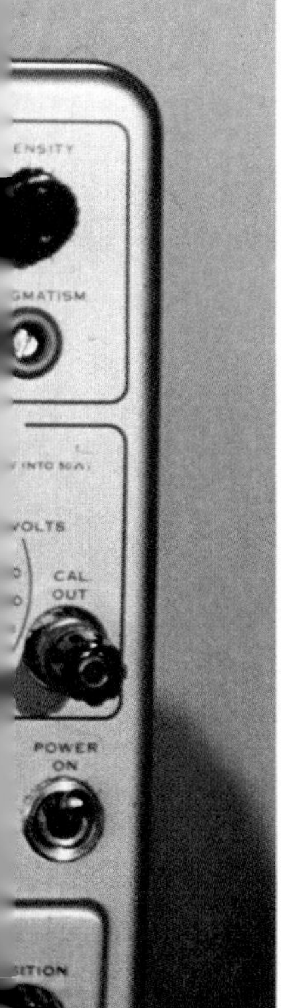

cranial self-stimulation or ICSS). ICSS shows promise in narcolepsy (a state of lethargy) and epilepsy (where the patient recognizes the 'aura' of an attack in time and inhibits it) and in relieving depression.

Many cultures have proclaimed the power of the mind over the body. A simple device now allows anyone who wants it to acquire conscious control of his 'involuntary' responses. The secret is simply to provide feedback of the particular function that is to be controlled. A watch and one's own finger on the pulse are all that is needed to learn in a few hours to slow or accelerate one's heartbeat. A sensitive electrical resistivity meter connecting two points on the subject's skin will provide feedback of his galvanic skin response (the reduction of skin resistivity by slight sweating), thus indicating the state of his sympathetic nervous system. With practice it is possible to learn to control the sympathetic response frequently associated with unease, agitation, anxiety, fear or fury.

A highly efficient artificial heart with its own perennial power plant is ready and waiting to be installed into the first human patient. From that moment on, heart transplant will be obsolete. By the year 2000 tens of thousands will be walking round with artificial hearts. The power source, then as now, will be a small amount of a highly radioactive isotope safely encased in a thick-walled metal capsule. (Safety considerations concerning the recovery and disposal of this substance after the patient's death are holding up installation at present.) The artificial heart powered in this way performs as well as an ordinary heart under normal conditions. It is far stronger, as a rule, than the diseased heart it replaces. At present, however, it cannot respond, as does a natural heart, to nerve impulses and hormonal messages requiring extra output. Whereas in a real emergency (such as having to run for your life) that is a drawback, most of the stimuli which accelerate heartbeat in our civilization do not really require the extra output, which only puts a strain on the rest of the system.

Artificial limbs will acquire enormous sophistication during the next 25 years. Like the heart, they will carry their own power systems, which can afford to be a good deal bulkier, heavier and stronger. They will be activated by a sensitive relay which picks up minute electric impulses from the nerve endings in the stump, thus putting their movements under the direct control of the nervous system, just like real limbs. Other artificial organs present even fewer problems: blood vessels, heart valves, ball and socket joints and bones are routinely repaired or replaced with synthetic materials today. The near future will see better replacements also for parts of the intestinal tract and for joints damaged by accidents or arthritis. Artificial teeth will soon be directly anchored in the jaw to last a lifetime. By 2000 tissues will be routinely transplanted, but few organs – perhaps only livers and kidneys. The liver is an incredibly complex organ, far beyond human ingenuity to create artificially. A single liver performs more chemical reactions every hour than all of the world's chemical factories combined. Many of these reactions are still beyond the capability of any chemical factory. Therefore, livers in good condition will be routinely removed from people who have died to be transplanted to people who would otherwise die. Kidneys are not nearly as complex as livers, and large machines can adequately rid the patient's body of waste products while he is hooked up to them. To miniaturize an artificial kidney sufficiently to implant it is probably a 21st century project. Until then there will be increasing use of kidney transplants. The list of tissue transplants is widening and will include teeth and bones. It will even be possible to grow a few cells from a patient in a tissue culture, and then give massive transplants of his own tissue back to him.

A simpler means to immortality is the sperm bank. A man looks at a nude while holding a container for the specimen he will shortly produce.

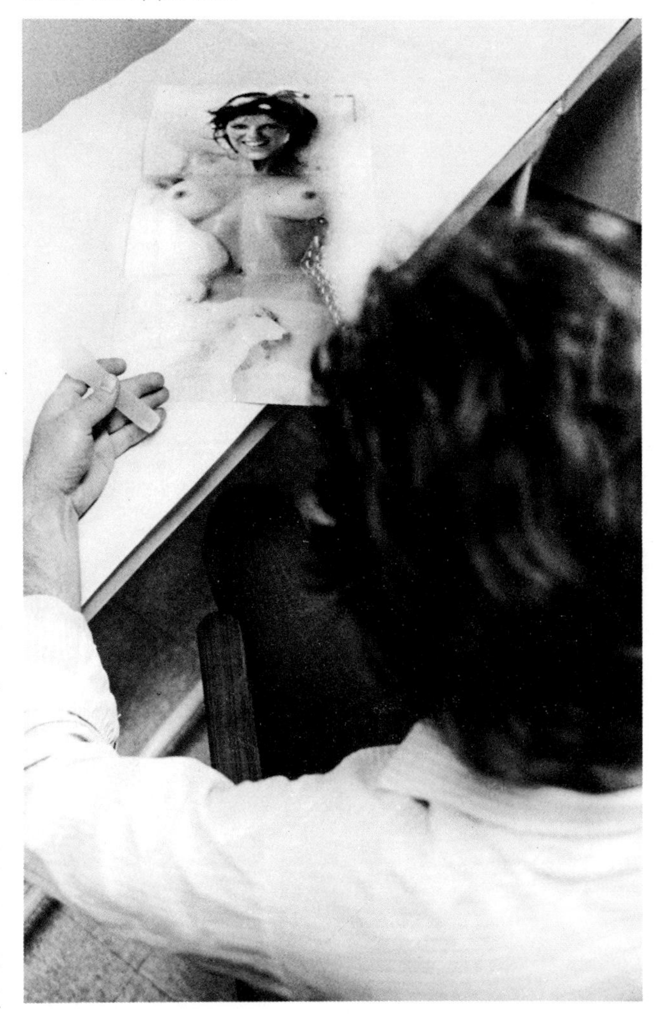

Even though transplanted retinas or inner ears cannot be linked to a recipient's brain, there is hope for the blind and the deaf. By the year 2000, most blind people will be equipped with electronic gadgets which enable

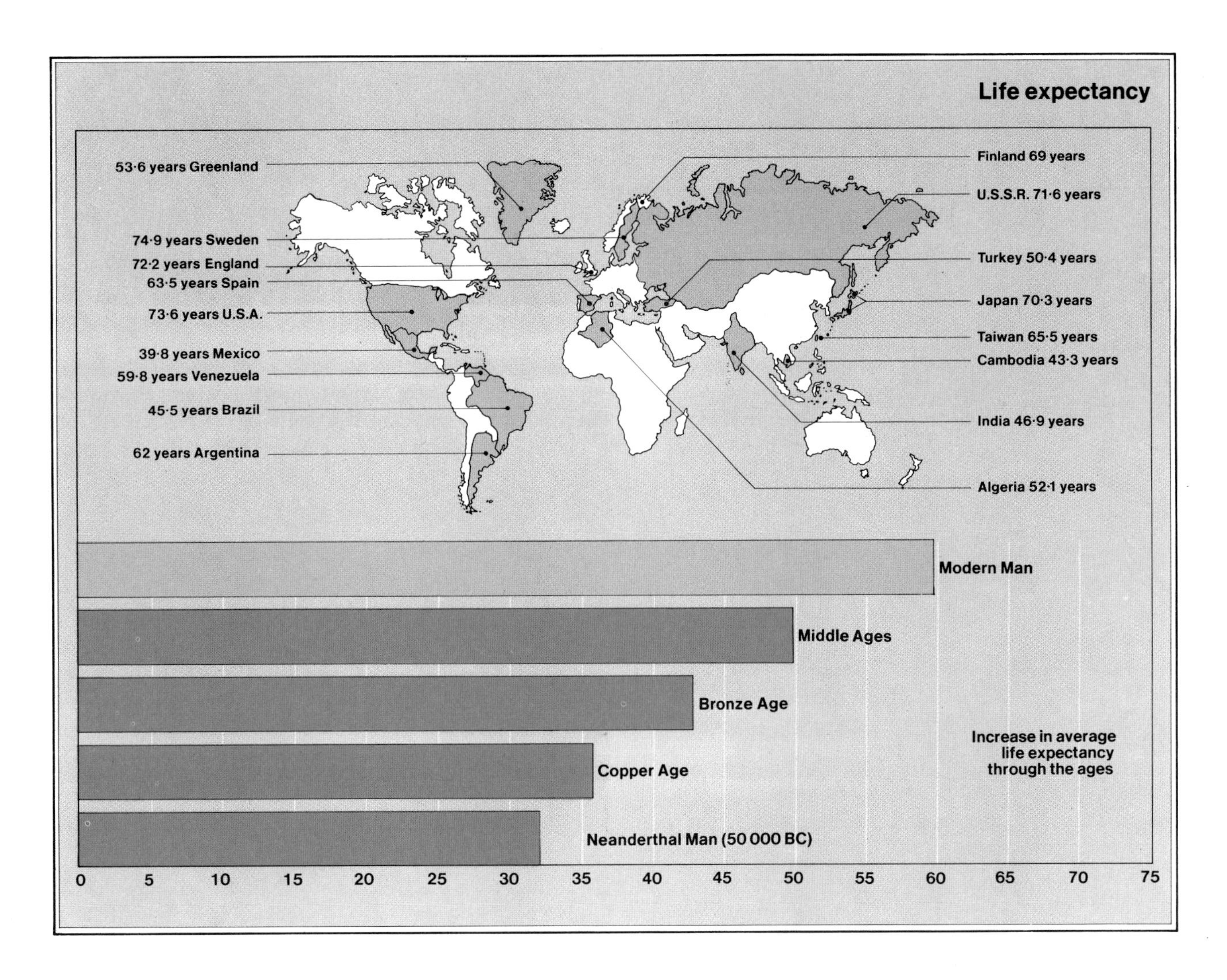

them to gather visual impressions of the surrounding world by means other than sight. A small television camera on the blind person's forehead could convert the received pattern of light and darkness into heat or cold impulses transmitted to an area of the chest so that he could interpret the sensations as objects and shapes. In the next decades blind people will undoubtedly be able to lead normal lives and even read at a distance.

To make the deaf follow conversations and speak is entirely feasible today and will be standard procedure soon. A battery-powered transistorized gadget the size of a small pack of cards can convert audio signals into luminous visual patterns it displays on its own little screen. Each sound corresponds to a different visual figure, which the deaf person soon learns to recognize and distinguish. By means of the feedback provided by the instrument he also learns to judge and recognize the sounds he himself produces. Given this instrument early enough he will learn to understand speech and speak himself at almost the same age as normal children.

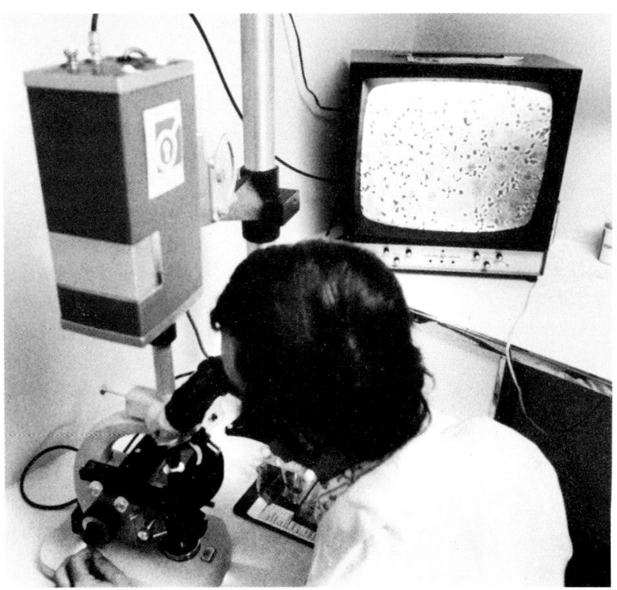

A technician examines a sperm specimen through a microscope. The image is projected onto a TV screen for a more exact study of quality and sperm count.

Man's resources

The resources which 20th century industrial man needs to maintain himself on earth can be divided into energies and materials. Man himself, however, is also a prime resource for it is through his knowledge and inventive capacities that resources are identified and exploited for his own purposes.

The energies that man exploits are stored energies – the fossil fuels, for example oil, coal and their gases, found in the earth's crust – and income energies from the sun and other sources. The stored energies are a finite non-renewable resource; the income energies are constantly renewed. Today man's use of industrial energies is a critical factor for the future of the developed and less developed parts of the world.

Between 1860 and 1960 the production of world energy increased by three per cent annually. But since 1960 this percentage has trebled because of the exponential growth of human populations and the increased rate of industrialization of agricultural regions. The industrial regions with about one quarter of the world's population consume 80 per cent of the natural gas produced, 75 per cent of the world's coal and 80 per cent of its oil. This means that an individual in the developed world regions consumes more than fifty times the industrial energy of his counterpart in the so-called poorer parts of the world. The paradox is that many of the raw materials and energy fuels used in the developed regions in fact come from the poorer ones.

With the present population increases and rates of industrialization man will require not double but up to five times more world energy by the year 2,000. This would mean an approximate 60 per cent rise per year in the overall use of fossil fuels. And if the non-industrial regions are to be industrialized to the same level as

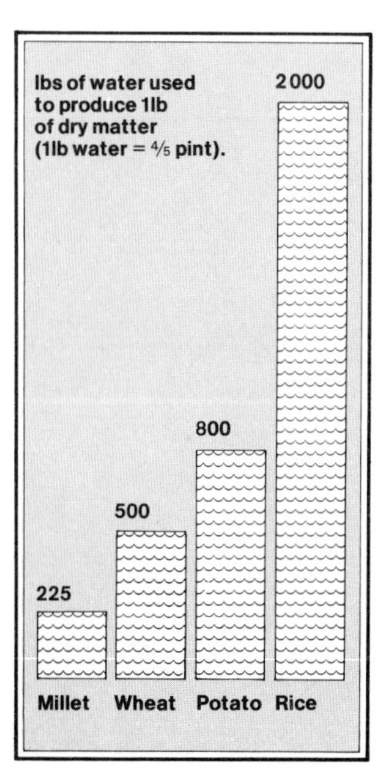

Palm trees' roots go down to underground water. To protect them from sand storms craters are formed round each cluster with a circle of palm leaves.

(Overpage) Project Tektite took place in 1969. Four aquanauts dived 50ft in a pair of steel tanks. Their goal was to stay 60 days under the sea.

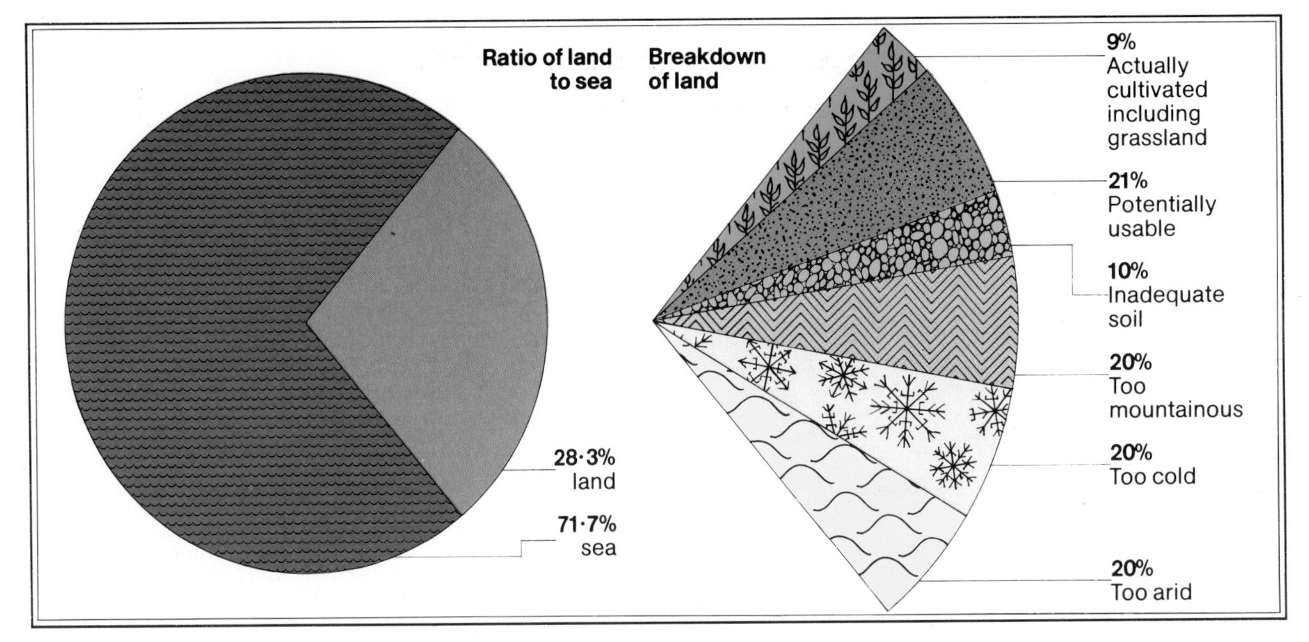

advanced countries this would result in an even greater demand. Within a hundred years present accessible reserves would be used up.

Of course man is not unaware of this problem. One obvious solution is to improve the technology of discovering new deposits. And major new discoveries have been made. In 1968 a 10 billion-barrel oilfield was discovered in Alaska. And there is evidence of large oil fields on the continental shelves and delta lands of south-east Asia.

Much has been said about nuclear power as the fuel source of the future. Since one pound of fissionable uranium is equal in energy to about 650 tons of coal, its energy production is far greater than that from any of the fossil fuels. And it has great advantages for the under-developed regions of the world: it can function anywhere; upkeep is minimal; operation is automatic and can be managed by limited personnel. But though as compared to present fossil fuels nuclear power is a clean source there still remains the problem of the disposal of radio-active wastes. However its emergence in the advanced regions of the world will probably accelerate solutions to this.

The exploitation of solar energy is being explored. As the annual solar radiation received by the earth is about 35,000 times our present yearly energy consumption the sun is comparable to a gigantic atomic reactor. Solar cookers and heaters are being developed. But so far the most successful use of solar energy has been aerospace work. The solar cell, converting sunlight directly into electric energy, has made possible much of the space exploratory data collected so far.

Other potential sources of (income) energy as yet unexplored are first the tidal movements of oceans into and out of coastal bays and river deltas; and second the hot springs which bubble out from the interior heat layers of the earth – these have added value as they are easily accessible.

Solar, water and tidal power are income energies – they are constantly being renewed. And it is these energies that industrial man must increasingly employ rather than the limited fossil fuels. Fossil fuels are not renewable and are too valuable to be used up in the current profligate way. They should be employed more carefully in indirect conversion to foodstuffs, plastics and other essentials.

In industrial societies in the 1970s the flow of materials and technologies is essential. Industrial raw materials are mostly found in the earth's crust – a ten mile thick shell of geologically formed deposits of metallic ores and non-metallic minerals. The eight elements of oxygen, silicon, aluminium, iron, calcium, sodium, potassium and magnesium make up 98·6 of the earth's crust. Other materials of great importance – nickel, tungsten and tin occur in much smaller quantities. The major concentrated deposits of these resources are distributed unevenly around the world. There is no part of the earth that is self-sufficient in all critical metals.

Two hundred years ago comparatively few metals were known to man. There were the noble metals – silver, gold and platinum – and the base metals – iron, lead, copper and tin. Although mercury was known it was hardly ever used. Brass and bronze were the main alloys.

With the arrival of the industrial revolution in the 19th century large scale production of metals began. In the first quarter of the 20th century more metal was extracted and processed than ever before and the quantity doubled in the succeeding 25 years. The bulk of this production was iron which was alloyed with small

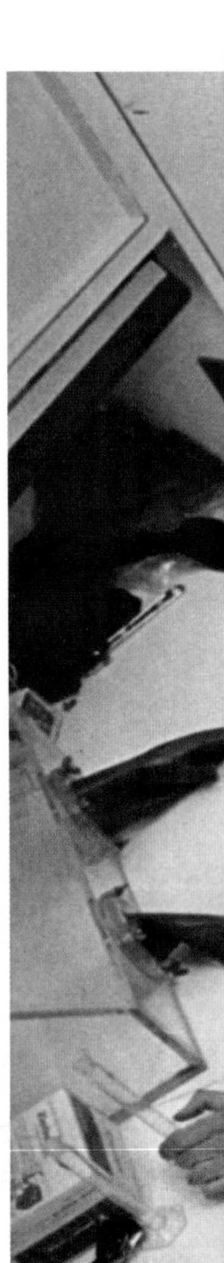

A mock-up of the USA's Rockwell Beaver 4 undergoing tests. The ship is designed to dive 2,000ft; cameras and lights are attached to the metal arms.

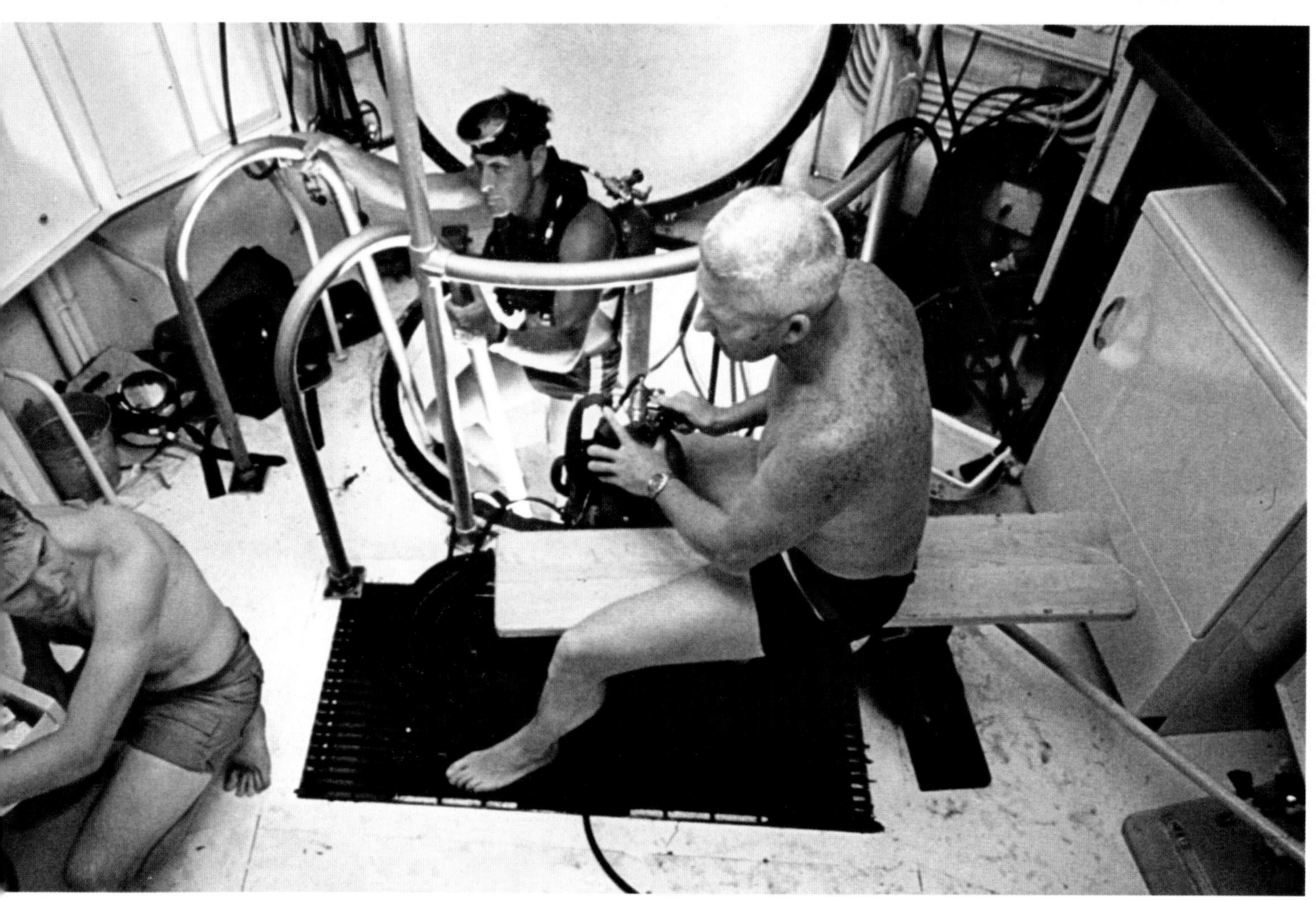

Life in the Tektite – the tanks were 18ft high, connected by a tube and jammed with equipment. It cost $1,500,000 to build.

A solar furnace catches the sun's rays via a huge mirror and produces energy which, unlike fossil fuels – coal etc – is constantly renewable.

At El Teniente in Chile – the world's largest copper mine – smoke pours out in the moonlight. Copper is expected to run out in 29 years time.

quantities of other metals to form a range of steel which, until the 1970s, has been the basis of our industrial civilization. Today we are moving towards a time when other metals, composite materials and plastics may well displace steel as the prime industrial material.

The only unique resource – as man makes advances in materials, research and energy production – is his own skill which enables him to convert one resource to another and to find renewable energy sources. If his skill can take him to the point where he has the capacity to restructure material resources to any desired range of physical properties, if he can produce energies in quantity from any locally preferred source he will be so close to nature's organic capabilities that he will have created a non-technology. Just as man is now living in a post-agricultural age he may arrive at a post-technological age.

Present technological advances are of course dependent on the amounts of metals available and metals are non-renewable. But given the facts that alloying chemistry can extend the number of their combinations and provide an increasing range of qualities; that metals and their alloys can be reused through scrapping; and that re-fabrication in different products means they are not used up or lost, the supply seems unthreatened. This relative inexhaustability however relies on a technology which uses less materials and less energies per function. The 'doing more with less' is an expression coined by R B Fuller who has pioneered the study of industry in terms of 'Dymaxion' principles – the gain of maximum physical advantage through minimal energy investment through constantly increasing 'performance per pound'.

Most analyses of other metal resources indicate the number of years' supply left in exploitable reserves. Aluminium, for example, 570 years; iron, 250; zinc, 23; copper, 29; lead, 19; tin 35. But these are misleading because they do not indicate the degree to which such metals are used up. Nearly all are highly recoverable through scrapping cycles – and can be used again and again. In fact in calculating the world's metal reserves we may include all those metals currently in use. And we can

In the effort to produce more food farming becomes more intensive. The prospect of soil erosion is a worrying problem for today's geoscientists.

even include those recoverable from the lowest grade ore deposits in the earth's crust, although we cannot, at present, economically exploit them. A real problem, however, is how less developed nations can be brought up to the level of materially advanced regions.

At present all industrial societies (with perhaps the exception of the USSR) import most of the metals and ores on which their economy depends. The United States, for example, is the world's largest consumer, with only six per cent of the world's population, consuming approximately 30 per cent of the total world production of minerals. At what point will the export of minerals by developing countries jeopardize their own chances of becoming industrialized?

To bring the total world population up to the same level of material consumption would, at a conservative estimate, require at least five times the present world production of minerals – far more than we can attain with present levels of materials and energies. The only hope for these under-advantaged countries is an overall world increase in the 'performance per pound' of all invested resources – doing more with less. The technology needed to achieve this is developing, but it must speed up and it must be used as a world plan. At some point in the future, man, by the use of massive supplies of nuclear energy may be able to extract endless supplies of minerals from the oceans and the earth's crust. He may also be able to construct or synthesize materials from many different element sources.

Man has of course already synthesized materials. Plastics were first used in the late 19th century but did not become widespread until 1927. Nearly every year since 1942 has seen the discovery of a new group of plastics. It is estimated that by the 1980s consumption of plastics will have overtaken that of iron products. Then there are composites – non-metal substitutes for metals which combine the properties of metals with those of ceramics and fibers in their forming and stress properties. Composites promise greater strengths than the theoretical limits of their separate constituents. And there are many others. It can only be a matter of time before many of our natural resources will be supplanted by laboratory substitutes. And with the new discoveries the less advantaged peoples of the world will be able to advance more swiftly. And indeed it would be better if these developing nations were to move straight into the new forms of industrial processes – synthetics, light metals, nuclear power generation and automated production. It is to be hoped that any questions as to how, what will it cost and who will pay will become increasingly irrelevant. Industrial man has already spent more in materials and energies than such a development would cost.

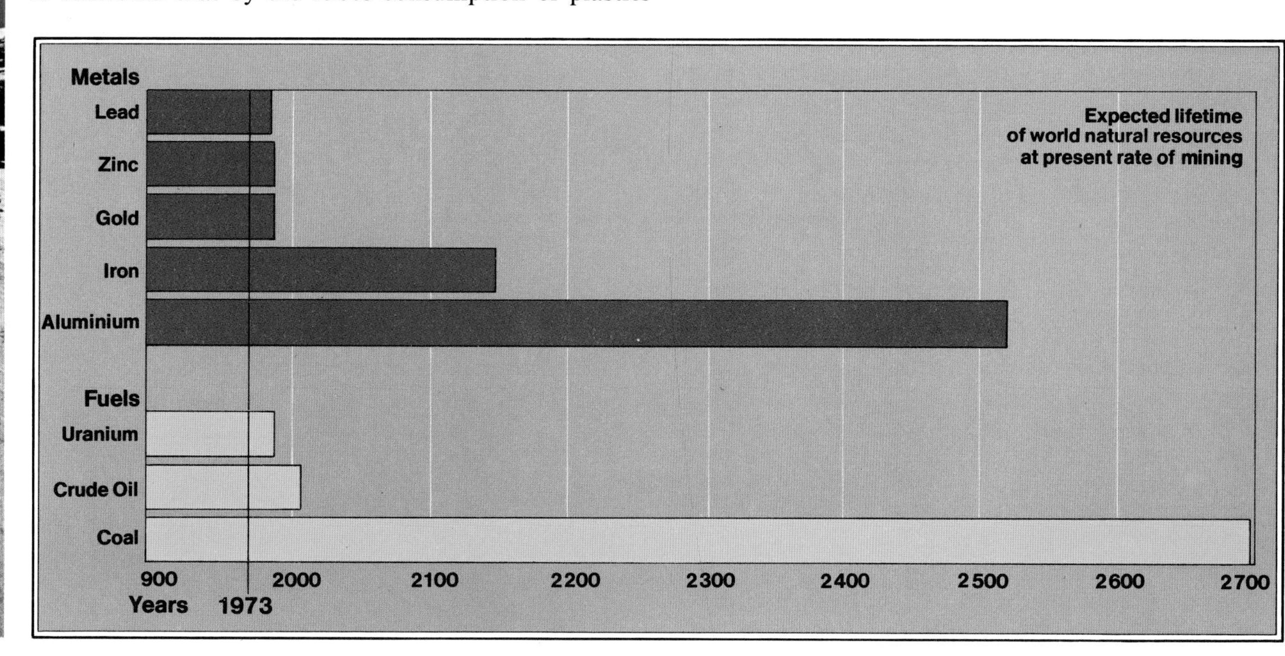

Man in space

The huge variety of questions and problems associated with space technology reflect many, if not most, of the questions and problems we associate with the future of life on earth. By removing ourselves from an earth-bound environment we are faced with all the difficulties of reproducing those conditions which support life on the earth. We learn of the most economic ways of utilizing power and other resources, discover techniques for recycling air, water and waste products, of regenerative food cycles, of miniaturization and sophistication of all aspects of our technology. What is known through physics is launched through space engineering. The problems of the future of life on earth can be recognized in the experiments we conduct in space. And yet the momentum of space technology is carried forward by a unique symbolism which veils its links with earth-bound technology.

In July 1969, less than ten years after John F Kennedy announced that his country would land a man on the moon before the end of the decade, a rocket stood on the launch pad at Cape Kennedy, Florida. For months the world had been murmuring of man's greatest adventure. Although many astronauts had already preceded this mission into space, no man had yet set foot upon the moon. And Saturn 5, standing there on the launch pad, towering 36 stories high with an Apollo spacecraft implanted on top of it, was to carry three men to the moon.

Saturn 5, the monumental and famous launch vehicle of the Apollo Program, had the sole objective of putting its little brother – the Apollo II space capsule – into a trans-lunar injection: that is, on the way to the moon. To this end, the rocket carried almost 6 million pounds of fuel. At lift-off it would deliver seven and a half million pounds of thrust, blasting itself, the size and weight of a naval destroyer, into the sky. Less than 18 minutes all told, the engines of Saturn would burn. Its third and last stage would achieve in a matter of minutes a velocity of 36,000 feet per second. With this it would escape the gravitational field of the earth. Certainly Saturn was capable of it, for the laws of physics demanded it. But in the history of rocket engineering, the practice had never been as clean or as certain. There were 50 years of rockets digging furrows in cornfields and catching fire on the pad from leaky valves to prove that.

But Saturn 5 made it off the ground, rivers of flame pouring hundreds of feet on every side. Seconds ahead of the apocalyptic fury of sound, it rose like a witch's hat above the white torch of the burn. It punched through the clouds, thousands of feet up, and over a PA system came the words 'at three minutes, downrange 70 miles, 43 miles high, velocity 9,300 feet per second'. But that was only the first stage. When that was burned out, it fell away and the second stage erupted, driving the rocket faster. Acceleration would continue until the second stage had been extinguished, and that only happened after Apollo-Saturn, traveling at 18,000 miles an hour

The astonishing extravagance of the Apollo Moon Program has been matched by its dramatic sophistication of all aspects of technology.

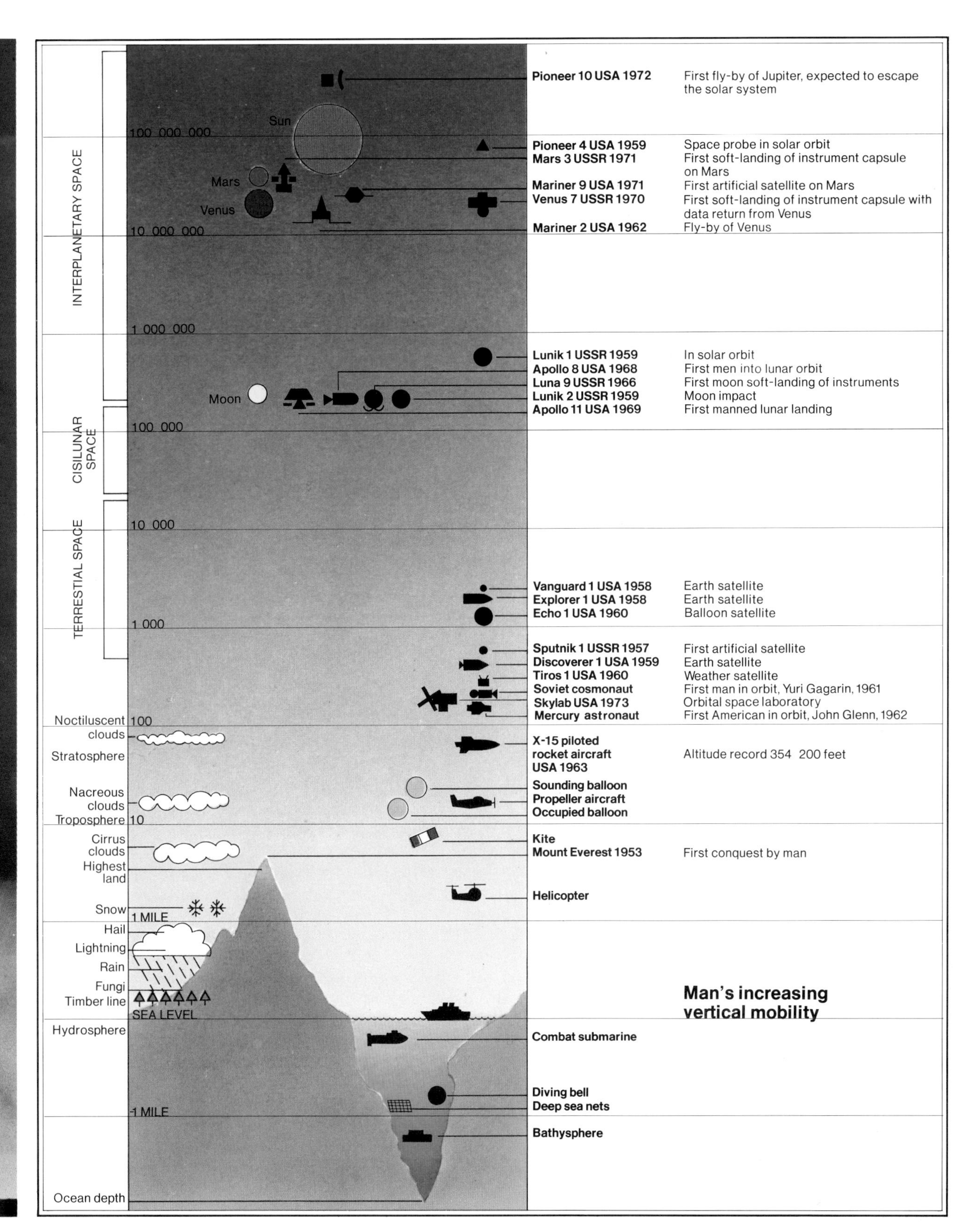

INTERPLANETARY SPACE
CISILUNAR SPACE
TERRESTIAL SPACE
100 000 000
10 000 000
1 000 000
100 000
10 000
1 000
100
10
1 MILE
SEA LEVEL
1 MILE
Sun
Mars
Venus
Moon
Noctiluscent clouds
Stratosphere
Nacreous clouds
Troposphere
Cirrus clouds
Highest land
Snow
Hail
Lightning
Rain
Fungi
Timber line
Hydrosphere
Ocean depth
Pioneer 10 USA 1972
First fly-by of Jupiter, expected to escape the solar system
Pioneer 4 USA 1959
Space probe in solar orbit
Mars 3 USSR 1971
First soft-landing of instrument capsule on Mars
Mariner 9 USA 1971
First artificial satellite on Mars
Venus 7 USSR 1970
First soft-landing of instrument capsule with data return from Venus
Mariner 2 USA 1962
Fly-by of Venus
Lunik 1 USSR 1959
In solar orbit
Apollo 8 USA 1968
First men into lunar orbit
Luna 9 USSR 1966
First moon soft-landing of instruments
Lunik 2 USSR 1959
Moon impact
Apollo 11 USA 1969
First manned lunar landing
Vanguard 1 USA 1958
Earth satellite
Explorer 1 USA 1958
Earth satellite
Echo 1 USA 1960
Balloon satellite
Sputnik 1 USSR 1957
First artificial satellite
Discoverer 1 USA 1959
Earth satellite
Tiros 1 USA 1960
Weather satellite
Soviet cosmonaut
First man in orbit, Yuri Gagarin, 1961
Skylab USA 1973
Orbital space laboratory
Mercury astronaut
First American in orbit, John Glenn, 1962
X-15 piloted rocket aircraft USA 1963
Altitude record 354 200 feet
Sounding balloon
Propeller aircraft
Occupied balloon
Kite
Mount Everest 1953
First conquest by man
Helicopter
Combat submarine
Diving bell
Deep sea nets
Bathysphere
Man's increasing vertical mobility

fell into an earth orbit. An orbit and a half would be spent testing out the infinitely complex communications systems and making checks on the conditions of the ship after the initial violence of the hurtle into space. Then finally it would make the break and head out across space for the moon. For that final dash it would need the full speed of some 25,000 miles an hour. And the third stage gave the rocket – now the brain on the end of a firecracker – that final boost.

Three days later Apollo is in moon orbit. Soon the three astronauts who accompanied Apollo on its mission look upon the moon's cratered surface. Three men, married to the massive technology of their spacecraft on which untold billions of dollars had been spent, who will become heroes. Only two actually landed on the moon's surface, but the idea in itself was heroic. In the same decade that the project had been conceived it was achieved. And the purifications of discipline and co-operation among technicians and the forces of technology that had gone into this achievement are probably the truest measure of this 'new age of man'. Two hundred and fifty thousand miles of hostile emptiness had been crossed to reach the moon, although that, of course, had been done before. Other men had already seen the dark side of the moon. It was those two astronauts' first steps on the surface that were so symbolic of this achievement.

As with most of man's conquests an orgy of self-congratulation might have followed. But there were also questions and even doubts. Was man's landing on the moon 'the noblest expression of a technological age, or the best evidence of its utter insanity?' There were few answers to this in the beginnings of the Apollo Program and the birth of NASA (the National Aeronautics and Space Administration) at the time when American prestige dropped because the Russians had put Sputnik into orbit around the earth. This was the first real entry into space and Soviet technology was then in some ways superior to American technology. For the Americans the trip to the moon became a dream, a new vision which might spur the nation forward. What better symbol could there have been for the technological age?

Neither Russia nor America stopped with the initial conquest of the moon. There were space flights to Mars and Venus that probed other inner parts of our universe, made apparently with little other motivation than exploration. The vision of the moon faded and while it was, to some degree, succeeded by other scientific and technological fascinations these were far less magnetic. Indeed, in America, there was even a cut-back in expenditure on space research. In 1973 the efforts of NASA seemed to be focused on space stations – known as *Skylab* – space shuttles and re-usable launch vehicles and on research into the effects of weightlessness, radiation and cosmic rays on astronauts.

Yet we may say with certainty that rocket engineering and space technology embody two of the most primitive and myserious actions of nature, harnessing the force of fire and the transmission of thought. Fire is used to hurl a rocket at the moon or any other planet; the thoughts of men are transmitted into electro-magnetic circuits which guide, control and preserve a spacecraft in its flight. The development and sophistication of these actions are the real rewards. Through the whole history of rocketry – during which some refused to burn, others died with horrible shrieks and another left nothing but a circle of ashes and afterwards it rained for eight days – it has been the vision of technicians to control these forces. And in the end, the motivation is clear. If man can direct himself through space, then he has duplicated in his spacecraft the conditions for life which the earth provides. He comes closer, in effect, to understanding his own ecology; he learns of the recyling of air, of water, of waste products, an experience – in miniature – of a closed, limited ecological system. Which, on a larger scale, is just what the earth is.

To some degree in America this experience may be seen as a by-product of focusing attention on how to put a man on the moon, how to evolve a technology (from the pure physics) sophisticated enough to do the job. After the fire on an earlier Apollo spacecraft – in which three astronauts died – America's vision of space research narrowed down to this single aim. But when the moment finally came, despite the huge jubilation, there was also a sense of anticlimax, as though it was only possible at that instant to recognize the true perspective of the event. It was one of the greatest steps ever taken by man, an arresting image of scientific and technological progress, but the nature of its value to mankind is difficult to understand. Paradoxically what is easier to understand is the wider implication of this success.

Almost every field of science and technology has been employed to transport and maintain man off the earth. This convergence of the sciences came at a time when man's self-conscious relationship with his own earth-bound environment was at a critical stage. In effect man launched a controlled experiment, not to discover the moon, but to determine how he may best use his science and technology in sustaining himself in a hostile environment assisted by all the refinements of control, communications and power. Solar energy, once the food only of plants, has been tethered to the spacecraft; man's physiology, his dietary needs, his psychology, all have been swept into the space research program for study.

In sustained space flights the closed ecology of the life-support system could be a model for the redesign of many large-scale industries whose waste products threaten to upset our whole environment. In both space flight and industry the problems of waste, re-use of materials, the recycling of clean air and water, are much the same. But the space flight is like a laboratory – the effects of mismanagement of any of these things are immediate. On earth mismanagement or malfunction sometimes takes years to detect. But, in addition, the space capsule is not planned merely for an astronaut's survival, but for the best conditions possible, the conditions in which he functions best. And it also goes beyond the wholly physical aspects, for if several astronauts are encapsulated together then their social relationships must be carefully guided towards the greatest co-operation. Multiple crew missions of long duration – planned in America with the *Skylab* program, and in Russia with similar space-station experiments – are effectively models of high density urban living.

In a space capsule the ideal system would be a completely regenerative, self-sustaining one in which water and oxygen would be recovered from the wastes; and air-conditioning temperature regulation, food preparation and disposal, sanitation and hygiene requirements would be linked in one integral system. At present the food cycle is the one that presents the most difficulties. But already NASA are projecting a regenerative 'closed loop' system which could maintain a nine-man crew on a 500-day planetary mission without resupply. This would cover the entire range of physical requirements, including waste management (which would be non-manual), personal hygiene, disposable and re-usable clothing and nutrition. In this project each crew member would have approximately 1,000 cubic feet of space in the module. And it could be said that what is actually being proposed is a prototype for an independently self-servicing house that could function anywhere on earth, without sewer lines or power inputs, or any other of the normal services.

The food cycle is perhaps the most obvious of all the problems shared by earth scientists and space researchers. The spaceman cannot rely on a food-production system which is not regenerative any more than can the exploding population of the earth. Duplication and miniaturization of the earth's food chain – through plant, animal, man, microbe and so on – is a far greater problem than that of water or air re-cycling. A recent approach is the chemosynthetic system, using microbes that take their energy from hydrogen rather than from light-conversion (as in the plant cycle) and are thus able to work in the dark.

This computer is part of a data-processing system which enables space engineers to predict satellite orbits even before they are launched.

Almost every aspect of space flight is simulated in advance. This chamber anticipates the effects of solar radiation on the spacecraft.

These theoretically edible organisms are composed of proteins, water, carbohydrates and fats. The Russians approached the idea of a carefully prógramed chicken battery, re-using processed wastes and algae to achieve an endless chicken supply.

Moon colonies, large space missions, even enclaves set up on other planets may demand new forms of social order. Men living so close together in isolated situations as these (reflecting the intensity of life in urban sprawls) are as rats to the sociologist. In communities on earth, stability and balance are emphasized in permanent human relationships; frustrations and aggravations can be released through various channels in the wide society. But a space colony would be a microcosm of society; there would be little room for releasing such emotions. In space it is essential that every person should be able to adapt himself swiftly to changes, and that these adaptations do not interfere with co-operative activities. A breakdown of social order as has occured in some urban communities would be instantly disastrous in space. And here it is interesting that the Russians put a woman into space quite early on. Women are regarded as better able to endure certain unfavorable conditions, like oxygen deficiency, but at the same time to have a nervous system which is more excitable and reacts more strongly to unusual situations. Overall the Russians have tended to emphasize more rigorous training for their cosmonauts, relying less on the tailored environment for their crews. But the questions are much the same. How do men or small groups cope with the isolation in space? What are the most effective forms of social relationships?

Two other questions have been current for decades, and these also reflect a concern for man's future on earth. Is there intelligent life elsewhere? Is it possible for humans to colonize other planets on a permanent basis? These questions verge on the fantasy of science-fiction, for the present state of our technology cannot provide the answers. In our solar system it is generally believed that life as we know it does not exist on any other planet, but it is possible that forms of life may be encountered through long-range communications with other solar systems. The possibility remains, however, that evidence of extinct life forms or past civilizations may be found on one of our planets. And there is the theory that man himself may have originated on other worlds, or at least that our original life form may have developed elsewhere.

The possibility that humans might be able to colonize another planet is not as unlikely as it may sound. On earth men have adapted to extreme environments with only the simplest of technologies to support them. The re-forming of extra-terrestrial bodies to maintain human life is obviously a task demanding vast amounts of energy and a far more sophisticated technology than we now possess – but the possibility remains, for the genius of man has always been in his ability to adapt both himself and his environment to his special needs.

The Apollo Lunar Module – which took three men to the moon – will not require basic redesign to carry men to other planets like Mars.

Index
Volumes I-XX

Index

Index

C

Index

Index

Index

Index

F

G

Index

Index

J

K

Index

M

Index

Q

Index

Index

U

V

W

Index

X

Y

Z